A BRIEF HISTORY OF

FORT WORTH

COWTOWN THROUGH THE YEARS

RITA COOK

Charleston | London

THE
History
PRESS

Published by The History Press
Charleston, SC 29403
www.historypress.net

Copyright © 2011 by Rita Cook
All rights reserved

First published 2011

Manufactured in the United States

ISBN 978.1.60949.175.8

Library of Congress Cataloging-in-Publication Data

Cook, Rita, 1964-
A brief history of Fort Worth : cowtown through the years / Rita Cook.
p. cm.
Includes bibliographical references and index.
ISBN 978-1-60949-175-8
1. Fort Worth (Tex.)--History. 2. Historic sites--Texas--Fort Worth. 3. Historic buildings-
Texas--Fort Worth. 4. Fort Worth (Tex.)--Buildings, structures, etc. 5. Fort Worth (Tex.)--
Biography. I. Title.
F394.F7C66 2011
976.4'531--dc22
2011012082

This book is dedicated to Baxter, Isabella and Seymour—friends forever!

CONTENTS

FOREWORD

I took a walk on the catwalk above the few cattle pens that are left here in the Fort Worth Stockyards and that are located just outside my Stockyards Museum office. The Stockyards Museum is operated by the North Fort Worth Historical Society, and both were founded by Charlie and Sue McCafferty. The McCaffertys saw the Stockyards diminishing right before their eyes, and they knew that they had to do something to preserve it. The North Fort Worth Historical Society was chartered in 1976.

Up on the catwalk, I looked across the area that used to be covered in pens but is now a parking lot. I looked straight down to the alleyways between the pens and saw the old original red bricks, the same ones the streets in the Stockyards are made from and that came from Thurber, Texas.

There are a few horses that belong to the hands that work the cattle drive and that are kept in the pens. And there is the small herd of longhorns that are used in the cattle drive. The cattle drive runs at 11:30 a.m. and 4:00 p.m. each day on Exchange Avenue in front of the Livestock Exchange Building.

These old buildings and pens hold a lot of history. The Livestock Exchange Building is 108 years old, and the Northside Coliseum is 102 years old. Even the bricks in the streets are historic!

While I stood on the catwalk, there was a spring-like breeze blowing, and I could hear the horses snorting, the birds singing, the steers bawling and the train whistling as it approached the Stockyards Station. I even heard the *clip-clop* of a horse and rider go by on the old red bricks below me. For a moment, I was transported back in time, and I could hear the sounds from one hundred years ago: cowboys yelling "git-up" and "yip-yip" to the cattle as they drive them down the alleyways to the Armour and Swift packing plants just up the hill, as well as the conversations of the cattle buyers as they inspect the different pens of cattle. I could hear the train approaching to bring in new herds to be sold.

The early spring wind blew the aroma of manure and horse flesh up to me, and the voices drifted on the wind with the Stockyards scent.

As I made my way down to the old pens, I touched the wooden gates, the bricks and the buildings, and I wished that they could talk. I wished that they could tell me the stories of the things they have seen.

It is through books such as this one by Rita Cook that we can read the pages, view the photos and hear the voices.

Teresa Burleson, director, Stockyards Museum
North Fort Worth Historical Society
Fort Worth, Texas

ACKNOWLEDGEMENTS

Thanks to my commissioning editor, Becky LeJeune. Also, a big thanks to the Stockyards Museum; the staff there not only furnished the photos for this book from Fort Worth's early days but were also always available for my many questions. A big thanks as well to the Fort Worth Convention and Visitors Bureau and to Leigh Lyons for helping me out when she could.

Finally, another big thanks to my husband and photographer, Russell William Dandridge, who took all of the photos in this book recapping the modern-day look of Fort Worth's Stockyards; through his lens, the past came alive.

Chapter 1

DISCOVERING FORT WORTH

The story of Fort Worth is really a story of the taming of north Texas. It's a story highlighting the role that one city played in the early Texas frontier days, and without Fort Worth, well, where would the West have begun? After all, Fort Worth is, in no uncertain terms, where the West really *did* begin—and that, we shall see, has been firmly rooted into the city's history.

All of the romantic notions come to mind when thinking of the early western cowboys; couple that with Indian fights and gunfights or, much later, cattle drives and rough and rowdy gangsters, and that's the real story. Later on, include those gushers that gave Texas oil its name and then, of course, the packing plants and railroads, assembly lines and today's ultramodern culture. It seems worlds away from those humble beginnings, but this is indeed the history of the city of Fort Worth.

One of the best things about visiting Fort Worth is the fact that you can still experience so much of the history everywhere. Throughout this book, we'll take a look at Fort Worth's beginnings and how it evolved as a city in the 1800s and 1900s, and we'll discover, too, that the city is still evolving. It's evolving, fortunately, while at the same time also embracing its past. Sure, while it's easy to stroll around Sundance Square or the Stockyards district and breathe in the present, the history you'll also encounter is a constant reminder that there is much in Fort Worth from the past that is well worth remembering today.

Fort Worth is a city of yesteryear but has always had one foot in the future, too. Fortunately, there is still much to do in Fort Worth relating to the West,

A recognizable bronze statue in the Stockyards area, 2011. *Photo by Russell William Dandridge.*

particularly in the Stockyards area or around the city as you admire the old buildings and homes. The image that Fort Worth once projected is still alive, and it is a good one for visitors to discover and for locals to enjoy.

Don't be fooled into thinking that Fort Worth was ever really just a one-horse town, either, because in addition to that popular "Cowtown" history, there's also a lot to see and do that will surprise you. In fact, the history involves, to a large extent, Fort Worth's early leaders, who took pride in shaping this place. After all, the city's museums are some of the best in the country. Where else are you going to find Warhol, Remington, Monet and Picasso in such proximity?

One might wonder how the city became such a metropolis, too, with all of the refined art, excellent restaurants and that subtle touch of southern class. The cowboys and oilmen who lived in Fort Worth in earlier times had the money to travel, and when they came back home from their sojourns, they brought big pieces of the world back with them—now seen in the art of the local museums and the culture embraced on every corner.

WHERE THE WEST BEGINS

Fort Worth is really *the* place to begin to take a look at the American West. It's the seventeenth-largest city in the United States and the fifth-largest city in the state of Texas. Bordering Dallas County and located in Tarrant County,

Fort Worth is on the very eastern edge of west Texas. In fact, "Where the West Begins" is the city's slogan and for good reason. Even with its size and its proximity to glittery Dallas, Fort Worth has not forgotten its roots—roots that are easily identifiable in not only the city's western heritage but also the lingering design and architecture that speaks of days gone by.

Established in 1849, the name "Fort Worth" holds a romantic ring just like it did in earlier times, even if that romance belonged to a bunch of rough-and-tumble cowboys in a, well, not-so-romantic time in our history.

When Fort Worth was first established in the mid-1800s, it began as a desolate outpost for the army, sitting on a bluff that overlooked the now popular Trinity River. Originally home to the Anadarko, Tonkawa and Waco Indian tribes, the land was fertile with game and water, and it was a good place to live, for both the Indians and settlers alike.

These days it is still a good place to visit or call home. With various areas around the city giving Fort Worth a good balance from the "cowtown" reputation that draws many visitors every year, there is also the distinguished cultural district west of downtown that offers some of the best art museums in the world. Whether you are interested in contemporary artists like Andy Warhol, western artists like Frederic Remington or the Old World masters such as Michelangelo, you will find it all in Fort Worth, thanks to the city's forefathers.

Also a step away from the past in Fort Worth is the Modern Art Museum, which houses the likes of Pollock among other well-known names, and the Fort Worth Museum of Science and History, which is home to everything from dinosaurs to diesel fuel. Performances abound in town, from country to opera to the symphony; it all depends on the day and your mood. In fact, Fort Worth's Sundance Square offers concerts and arts performances that many say are some of the best west of the Mississippi.

The Stockyards National Historic District has always been a big draw for tourists and locals for many different reasons. These days, there are a number of daily historic events, with the most notable being the twice-daily cattle drive along the city street in the Stockyards area. It is the only one in the world of its kind. You've seen it in the movies, but in Fort Worth you can see it live.

The history held today in Fort Worth was a hard-earned history, and many stories relate to the earlier days on the frontier—it is where the West was won, too. From the cowboys and cattle drives that you can still envision on the streets to the railroad building and Hell's Half Acre—a gritty place that earned its name—it's all about the stimulating beginnings of a city whose

Left: The always popular cattle drive in the Stockyards, 2011. *Photo by Russell William Dandridge.*

Below: Cattle being driven through the Stockyards area in Fort Worth, which happens daily, 2011. *Photo by Russell William Dandridge.*

rugged pioneers left a legacy that still lives on today in the heart and soul of the city of Fort Worth.

Fort Worth's designation as the place where the West began was due especially to the city's association with the Chisolm Trail, a route used by the ranchers and cowhands to drive their cattle north. It wasn't long, then, before this route helped establish Fort Worth as a trading and cattle center in the Southwest. But so much more went into it, and it was the city's ability to build on its past that gave it the future both in the last century and today.

With the Chisolm Trail, it was proper that little Fort Worth would become known by its still popular nickname, "Cowtown." The cowboys stopping over in Fort Worth made sure that they had their fill before the long road ahead of them up north, with the large herds of cattle they were driving out of Texas. From necessary supplies to enjoying the town's colorful saloons, gambling and carousing, the Cowtown reference was certainly a well-earned name for Fort Worth, and the locals now take pride in the designation, blending the cattle and the more recent oil heritage with a laid-back vibe you'll feel in the city today.

A cowboy rides in front of Texas Cowboy Hall of Fame, 2011. *Photo by Russell William Dandridge.*

Of course, as the city is still a cowboy mecca, every Friday and Saturday night there are always a number of nationally ranked cowboys who ride bulls at the Stockyards Championship Rodeo at Cowtown Coliseum. Bringing the past into the future, too, is the Sterquell Wagon Collection at the Texas Cowboy Hall of Fame and the world-famous honky-tonk Billy Bob's Texas, located in Fort Worth. So pull out those cowboy boots and get ready to dance.

THE FIRST SETTLEMENT

It was actually in the winter of 1840 that the first settlement really began in the Fort Worth area, near today's town of Birdville. Sam Houston came through in 1843 to meet with a number of Indian chiefs in the area from different local tribes with a plan to discuss a peace treaty. Eventually worked out between the chiefs after Houston's departure, he left General H. Tarrant and George W. Terrell in charge of dealing with the chiefs, and when the tribes did come to the table to discuss the terms, a treaty was decided in which the local Native Americans would remain west of a line that is now Fort Worth. The line was marked "Where the West Begins," and that is where the city got its famous slogan.

The 1840s saw many Americans moving west and away from the East Coast. With the rush of settlers moving into the area, the Native Americans were pushed back even farther and were forced to find new hunting grounds. However, like in other parts of the West, it wasn't the Native Americans giving these new settlers a hard time but rather the tensions building with Mexico to the south. The tensions had been rising for some time between the then republic of Texas and Mexico—it had only been a few years since Texas had won victory in 1836.

In December 1845, the republic of Texas became the twenty-eighth state of the United States of America, and with that the American army got involved in the Texas and Mexico scuffle, too. With blood being shed in April 1846, Congress declared war on Mexico.

What did this have to do with Fort Worth particularly? It was mainly because of the involvement of a man named General William Jenkins Worth, who was second in command at the beginning of the war and very involved in the entire situation. Of more importance, after much fighting with Mexico in 1849, Worth asked for a line of ten forts that would indicate the western Texas frontier line, with forts to be placed in areas from Eagle Pass in south Texas to the Trinity River near Fort Worth. While he died soon after his proposal, Worth's idea did come to light, with the city of Fort Worth being named after him because of his obvious forward thinking. When Worth died, a general named William S. Harney took his place and commissioned his men to find a fort site in the area; the camp was then soon established on the bank of the Trinity River and named Camp Worth in honor of General Worth. While the fort was actually moved to the north side overlooking the fork of the Trinity River, the name was officially designated as Fort Worth in November 1849.

However, records indicate that for the troops living at Fort Worth back in the latter part of the 1840s, not much excitement was to be found, even if they were slightly inside Indian territory. With great views in the summer on the bluff of the river, though, the winters did not prove quite as accommodating, with snow and sleet at times making for a bleak existence—after all, those Texas summers could get hot, just as hot as the winters got cold. Due to these reasons, there were actually as many as thirty or more men who deserted the fort during this time.

As for the Native Americans in the area, they didn't turn out to ever be much of a threat, and mainly only the few curious ones looking to trade came through the area. Sure there might have been a few minor skirmishes, including one that was recorded, but it turned out in the long run that most "wild Indian" stories were simply myths. The most popular story was one in which a local Comanche band in the area were causing trouble, particularly Chief Jim Ned and Feathertail, both of whom had supposedly decided that Fort Worth was in the way of their old hunting grounds. The soldiers were called in. The story goes, however, that this skirmish turned out to be only partially true at best. What is true is that the soldiers living at the fort were often wondering if hostile attacks might be just around the corner, though none ever was.

The real success of the fort actually came when it was abandoned in 1853; up until that point, there had been a law passed that prohibited shops to be established within a mile of the old fort, thus when the fort was abandoned businesses were able to move in closer to the once busy structure. With this move, the town was officially on its way to becoming a real possibility, and it came complete with the name of Fort Worth already intact.

In fact, locals took advantage of every part of the fort, the army's onetime stable became the home for a hotel and bar, the soldiers' sleeping area became a general store and the officer's quarters was the perfect first home for the town's doctor, Carroll M. Peak. The preexisting barracks hospital became the first school, run by a man from Kentucky named John Peter Smith (a name still recognized in Fort Worth today, as he is often referred to as the father of Fort Worth). He eventually took part in local politics, making a big difference to the city's growth over time. Out of the old parade ground area in the fort a town square was made, and with a number of roads already forged by many a military man, the route to west Texas was already established. Even better, Fort Worth was the perfect "last stop" before the wilderness that lay ahead for any travelers heading north.

Today, there is no trace of the fort that once stood, but the city itself is a true memorial to General Worth's foresight and courage. Originally, the settlements that established the city proper included Alton, Birdville and Grapevine in 1849. A group called the Peters Colony was the first to get permission to homestead on the land located in Fort Worth, but while many of the Native Americans had been pushed back from the onslaught of settlers, there was still the fear and the danger that there could be attacks. Therefore a place called Johnson Station was also built, which at the time offered settlers a fair amount of protection via local rangers should there be the never-realized Indian attacks that most settlers feared.

FORT WORTH KEEPS GROWING

Fort Worth also saw its share of protecting colonists. The city was strongly affected by the Civil War. In fact, the city's courthouse had to stop construction after being started in 1859 because of the onslaught of the war.

Folks like Butch Cassidy and the Sundance Kid also came through the area. In fact, Sundance Square in downtown Fort Worth was named after the Sundance Kid. Many folks have heard of the legendary Hell's Half Acre in Fort Worth; with the outlaws and rowdy cowboys, it is safe to say that the place earned its reputation fair and square.

Fort Worth was eventually named the county seat for Tarrant County, but even way back in 1856, the little community on the Trinity River had its eye on the county seat, eventually taking it away from Birdville—in what some called a "stolen" election—through the use of good whiskey and padding the vote count. It was in 1856 that the first post office was opened in the area, and a stagecoach route was established between Fort Worth and Jacksboro; with these important additions, Fort Worth established itself even more as a town with a future.

At the perfect location with regard to the old Chisholm Trail, Fort Worth drew ranchers and cattle hands almost from the very beginning, easily giving the city a reputation and a name that it still lives up to today.

With its brush with the Civil War, Texas was also the destination of choice for many disenchanted Confederate soldiers who saw the state as the perfect place to find a job and start over again. That said, the North was hungry, and Texas had a good supply of cattle to supply up north, another plus for what this town in the Southwest had to offer to the rest of the nation.

However, the Civil War had also left a true need for reconstruction in Texas, and with Dallas taking on the role of a financial center, Fort Worth decided to keep to its western roots with an eye toward the number of cattle still on the plains, as well as the ranchers and frontiersmen still in need of homes. During this time, while many were looking at the West as useless and forgotten, the cowboys and cattle barons saw money and opportunity and took advantage of it, giving Fort Worth a chance to emerge as just the right place to be—the true West not in the making but rather already made. Indeed, with new cattle trails forged from Texas to Kansas and even Montana, it all started in Cowtown down south.

By 1868, the courthouse was finally finished and a big feather in the town's cap now, but it seemed that Fort Worth was still only a blur to many cattlemen, so something had to be done in order for the city to be noticed. Fort Worth needed more notoriety. So the next step was obviously for the residents to offer travelers amenities.

And so, Fort Worth had gotten itself together enough by 1873 to have a number of hotels and restaurants established by this time, as well as, of course, a number of gaming houses that kept the cowboys and frontiersmen happy, too. Shops offered dry goods, hardware, leather goods and even ice, and soon blacksmiths, printers and even a photographer moved in, along with a group of professional businessmen such as attorneys, doctors and even bankers and clergymen.

Speaking of clergymen, the local churches during this time in Fort Worth had more of a lean toward the Protestant way than anything else, yet a healthy number of Catholics and Episcopalians had also found their ways to the city, and all were living in harmony. With twenty schools, which were mostly just one-room buildings, it is also noted that weekly newspapers were popular by this time. In 1872, the *Fort Worth Democrat* was established, helping to grow the city the same way that the *Fort Worth Star Telegram* would do years later, established by Amon Carter.

In 1873, leaders of Fort Worth decided to apply to the State of Texas for a city charter, and on March 1, the city was given this right to charter, encompassing four square miles that included the bluff over the Trinity River. By this time, too, Fort Worth had already taken on a personality that would easily help catapult it into the future, with a mayor-alderman form of government. The city lacked only one thing it really needed now, and even that didn't take too long to be introduced, effectively putting Fort Worth on the map: a railroad.

The railroad was on the verge of arriving by the mid-1870s, and the Texas & Pacific Railroad finally did make it to Fort Worth in 1876, a move that had a huge impact on the cattle industry, too. For one, Fort Worth was located the farthest west than any other cattle town and was a good shipping point, especially with the use of the railroad. The railroad, therefore, gave Fort Worth exactly what it needed as a legitimate place to do business for any smart-minded businessman or cattleman.

Soon, however, parts of Fort Worth became downright dangerous, and it's no surprise that the likes of gunmen and outlaws ended up in Fort Worth at one time or another. In fact, after a few notorious robberies, the "Wild Bunch" of outlaws all came through Fort Worth and were able to easily lay low without being caught in Hell's Half Acre. Indeed, inside this dangerous Fort Worth area Butch Cassidy and the Sundance Kid supposedly had a good

An outlaw family house that is now the Jim Lanes Office at 204 West Central, 1930s. *Courtesy of the Stockyards Museum.*

The Stockyards Hotel is still in operation, 2011. *Photo by Russell William Dandridge.*

time hanging out, and one outlaw even wrote, "We rented an apartment and were living in style." So comfortable in their new surroundings were the Wild Bunch—Harry Longbaugh (the Sundance Kid), Ben Kilpatrick, Jim Lowe (Butch Cassidy), William Carver and Harvey Logan (Kid Curry)—that they walked around by day, enjoying the saloons and gambling halls. Reports tell one story of the five men even walking into a portrait studio to sit for a portrait, but it was a bad move since that photo was then turned into thousands of wanted posters. To that effect, the men got smart and left town before they were discovered. It was the last hurrah for the legend of the outlaw in Fort Worth in the early 1900s.

Indeed, the Stockyards area was a rough-and-tumble place back in the early days of the cowboy, but there was one area that took advantage of this clientele then and still does today: the Stockyards Hotel, which was established in 1907 and can famously say that even Bonnie and Clyde stayed there during their careers as outlaws.

Since "Cowtown" was so named, the Stockyards Hotel has played host to cowboys, cattle barons, outlaws and, more recently, kings and queens of country music as well. Going back in time is easy in many of Fort Worth's establishments, and a stop-in at the famous hotel is just the beginning of the ongoing story of the city of Fort Worth.

Chapter 2

THE IMPORTANCE OF
THE 1800S

After the initial establishment of the fort, along with the small town that had grown up around it, and after the troops moved out, it was just a matter of time before Fort Worth locals found what they needed to do to survive. After all, with so many settlers having moved into the area, it was obvious that the town could only prosper, and it wasn't long before folks soon began to establish schools, stores and churches.

Delving a little deeper into Fort Worth's humble beginnings, it was the town of Birdville, which was the largest town in the area and the seat of Tarrant County in the 1850s, that became really upset when Fort Worth finally did set its mind on becoming a real city of substance. As it was noted earlier, it didn't take long for the folks in Fort Worth to take that county seat designation away from Birdville. With the folks in Fort Worth being serious about this, a courthouse election was called, and Fort Worth got what it wanted—but, as many say, it wasn't fair and square. In fact, there was a barrel of Birdville's whiskey put into play to swing the vote, as the story goes. It was a barrel of whiskey that was actually to be used on election day, but it was found out by the folks from Fort Worth, siphoned, taken to Fort Worth and given to voters. Fort Worth won the narrow election for the county seat, and Birdville folks ended up bitterly accusing some men not even living in the county to have voted in the election. Of course, the men being accused had voted for Fort Worth.

Soon after the new county seat was established, folks moved to the town in droves. The city had its first postmaster, pioneer settler Captain Julian Field, who also opened a flour and corn mill. Captain Ephraim Daggett opened the

The Stock Exchange Building, 1903. *Courtesy of the Stockyards Museum.*

first hotel, the aforementioned Dr. Carroll Peak was the town's first physician and John Peter Smith opened the first school. There was also a slew of folks coming through and opening new churches, and in 1873, with just five hundred residents, the city was incorporated and elected its first mayor, Dr. W.P. Burts.

Now an established town, the late 1800s brought not only the outlaws and rowdies who gave Fort Worth much of its personality but also a group of folks looking for and eventually establishing a more stable community. In part, this had to do with the railroad, since it brought in more jobs and people to work in the meatpacking plants, the brewing companies, the newspapers and even the strong banking system in the town.

With a need for security as more people showed up, Fort Worth leaders modernized the fire department and gave Fort Worth a municipal water system, sewers and even some paved roads. Public schools were soon legalized in Texas, and colleges were soon to follow, of which there are still quite a few left in the city today.

In fact, Texas Christian University, still in existence today, was founded during the nineteenth-century Christian Restoration Movement by Joseph Addison Clark (1815–1901) and sons Addison (1842–1911) and Randolph (1844–1935). Clark came to Texas in 1839 and was a teacher, preacher, lawyer, surveyor, editor and publisher, and he was also the Fort Worth postmaster during the cattle trail era. When his sons came home from the Civil War, they established a school. Over time and moving to various locations, the school ended up in Waco but was renamed Texas Christian University in 1902. It finally moved to Fort Worth after the Waco main building was destroyed by fire in 1910. Fort Worth offered the school fifty-two acres of land for a campus and funds of $200,000 for building in the city.

It was in 1907 that the Texas legislature outlawed gambling, but with many other more honorable professions having come to Fort Worth by now, the city didn't look back and quickly became known for meatpacking, actually becoming the center of it all for the entire Southwest area. Of course, this also had to do with the fact that cattle being moved north almost always made a stop in Fort Worth in the 1800s. Even better, men moving their cattle meant that women often accompanied their husbands, and this led to a need for more shopping in Fort Worth.

Not enough can be said about the fact that the railroad played a huge part in the success of Fort Worth in the 1800s. With the Texas & Pacific Railroad (T&P) constructed westward across the state of Texas, it didn't take long for it to arrive in Fort Worth, and when it did it brought in even money and a need for commerce.

A man named Captain B.B. Paddock will always be remembered in Fort Worth. A Civil War veteran, he became the editor of the city's first important newspaper, the *Fort Worth Democrat*. His position as editor and his excitement for the upcoming railroad to the city meant that folks had a bird's-eye view of the railroad happenings. He published a map on the paper's masthead indicating where the nine railroads would enter Fort Worth—this before the railroad had even arrived, too, but he got folks excited anyway.

By 1872, the railroad had made it six miles west of Dallas, but that's when the problems actually began for Fort Worth—a disaster really, because the Wall Street firm that had been taking financial responsibility for the railroad decided to back out. People soon left Fort Worth in droves because the railroad wasn't coming, and the population actually dropped from four thousand to under one thousand in no time.

More resilient than that, however, Fort Worth wasn't ready to give up, and even though the city was all but deserted by now, there were still some folks who believed. One morning, a remaining citizen started a rumor that a panther had come into town and slept in the street since there were virtually no people left living and sleeping there. It got the rumors started, though, and folks were talking about Fort Worth again; consequently that's how Fort Worth ended up with another of its nicknames, "Panther City."

Fort Worth was deserted, maybe, but not to be discouraged, the Fort Worthians still living there decided that if the railroad didn't come to them, they would go to the railroad. Folks began building the line themselves under the name the Tarrant County Construction Company. According to some historians, one man gets special mention for his involvement in the project: Major K.M. van Zandt. He was a lawyer and was fresh from the Confederate army. He had moved to Fort Worth in 1865. It was Van Zandt, as well as a Captain E.M. Daggett, Thomas J. Jennings and H.G. Hendricks, who gave the railroad company 320 acres in the south of the city, and then Van Zandt was elected president of the construction company, too.

A few more problems still lay in the way of the railroad coming to Fort Worth. For example, in order not to lose the state land grant that the city had been given, the railroad had to reach Fort Worth before the legislature adjourned that year. Needless to say, not everyone in the legislature was for the railroad making it to Fort Worth, either, and it is noted that some representatives tried to end the legislative session early just for that reason. In the end, it was down to two days to complete the tracks, but the men worked day and night to make sure that the future of Fort Worth was secured. And it was!

With much excitement, the first train into Fort Worth chugged in on July 19, 1876. The victory had been won, and now Fort Worth could be a shipping point to destinations farther north. Cattle pens were built in anticipation, and with the railroad the stagecoach also began a route from Fort Worth to San Angelo.

Furthering the success of the stagecoach even more, on August 15, 1878, the post office opted for a route from Fort Worth to Fort Yuma in Arizona called Star Post Route No. 31454. This route was opened under contract to J.T. Chidester. Stagecoaches carried the mail along much the same route used by the Butterfield Overland Mail in the late 1850s. Fort Worth–Yuma mail was discontinued after completion of the southern transcontinental railroad in 1881, but during its run the distance was 1,500 miles, and it was the longest daily stagecoach line to run during that time. In fact, it took almost two weeks to make the run, and due to danger along the way, it also required escorts. The trail still exists, too, and can be found on Spur 520 and IH820 in Fort Worth.

With railroads and stagecoaches, Fort Worth added its first streetcar in 1876, running from the courthouse to the train station, with the service being pulled by mule-drawn cars. More progress was made when, in the late 1870s, elevators were invented, and Fort Worth was able to establish a grain center. In 1882, a man named M.P. Begley, the son of a Kentuckian, established a flour mill in the city, which held up to fifty barrels per day.

In 1886, the city saw its first Stock Show, and the show continued to grow over the years to much success and changing locations, but even so the Stock Show rodeo was the first to be held indoors. It has become a model for other rodeos around the world.

Trolleys in front of the Swift plant, 1905. *Courtesy of the Stockyards Museum.*

The year 1876 saw the first well being drilled, giving Fort Worth its drinking water. After that, it didn't take long before water lines were also laid. The streets from the courthouse to the train station called Main and Houston were paved, bridges constructed and even a fire department put into place, all a part of a thriving new city that was quickly moving forward.

Another strong factor in Fort Worth's success came with the onslaught of bankers moving into town, from Captain Martin B. Loyd, who opened in 1870 an "exchange office" that became the First National Bank in 1877, to a private bank being opened in 1873 by Thomas A. Tidball and John Wilson and even to Major van Zandt, John Peter Smith and Major J.J. Jarvis, who took interest in the same bank the following year, with the name changed to Tidball, Van Zandt and Company. Other names and hands changed in Fort Worth's banking industry as the 1800s drew to a close, with new names like the Fort Worth National Bank and the Continental National Bank, established in 1903, which was one of the first banks to lend money for oil development.

The 1880s were also a wild time in Fort Worth, with gunfighters slinging through town for excitement, like the presence of James Courtright, a six-gun shooter who was also a city marshal and someone no one wanted to mess with—he could shoot with either hand equally well and knew what

The White Elephant Saloon, 2011. *Photo by Russell William Dandridge.*

he was doing. Since he was so notorious, he managed to convince all of the saloon and gambling hall owners that they needed his protection in the wild Fort Worth frontier or else there would be trouble. Most folks acquiesced to his suggestion, with the exception of the owner of the White Elephant Saloon, a situation that did not end well. Eventually, there was a gunfight between the White Elephant Saloon owner and Courtright; legend has it that Courtright had the longest funeral procession in the history of the city.

Other firsts that quickly changed the landscape of Cowtown included, in 1881, the first telephone exchange in the city, with only a mere forty customers. In 1885, electric lights appeared, and in 1889 the Texas Spring Palace was opened, a two-story structure with eight towers and a dome.

However, in the spring of 1890, a fire broke out at the hall, and thousands of folks already inside ran for the door to get away from the fire that had started on the second floor. The fire burned quickly since the decorations in the hall were flammable, but the fire department worked fast, and everyone except one person made it to safety. The man who died was a civil engineer who had been helping folks out of the burning building. His name was Al Hayne, and a monument was erected in Fort Worth that can still be seen today in honor of his bravery.

The Stockyards Station is a newer addition to the Stockyards area, 2011. *Photo by Russell William Dandridge.*

Then and now, the Stockyards have always played a significant role in Fort Worth, and today you can visit the area on any given day and find a crowd. A few places that take history to the next level, places that really outline the lively 1800s, include the museum and Stockyards Station Gallery, and both are "musts" on the list of history stops in Cowtown.

Chapter 3

SIGNIFICANCE OF FORT WORTH ON THE OLD CHISHOLM TRAIL AND THE STOCKYARDS

The Stockyards entrance sign in the background of the historical Fort Worth destination is a landmark structure that was built in 1910. The huge columns supporting the sign were quite an accomplishment for the time. It was a sight for the road-weary cowboys and frontiersmen, Fort Worth being the last stop on a major longhorn cattle drive up the Chisholm Trail to the railheads. Rest and supplies before the long drive ahead were what Fort Worth was all about—before crossing the Red River into Indian territory, which also came along with many unknowns around every corner. It made Fort Worth look awfully good to these weary men as the last stop.

Fort Worth's Eastern Cattle Trail can still be seen today and is a designated National Historic Landmark in Heritage Park. The native stone, dug from the Trinity River Valley, marks the route of the Eastern Cattle Trail, where cattle were driven north on Rusk Street (present-day Commerce Street) through the city of Fort Worth and then to the bluff and across the Trinity River to the valley below, before resting and heading north.

In fact, from the end of the Civil War to 1876, when the railroad came through, many herds of cattle passed on this trail to Abilene, Kansas. The Eastern Trail, also called the McCoy Trail, is the route that becomes the Chisholm Trail when it reaches the Red River.

First things first, however: what was the Chisholm Trail and why was it important to Fort Worth overall? A Scotch-Cherokee trader by the name of Jesse Chisholm was the person who first marked the trail in 1864 for his wagons. The trail began at the meeting place of the Little and Big Arkansas Rivers and headed toward the southwest part of what is now Oklahoma City.

The Feeders and Breeders Show, with men and steers in pens, 1910. *Courtesy of the Stockyards Museum.*

Fort Worth's Stockyards sign shows the Stockyards is still alive and well, 2011. *Photo by Russell William Dandridge.*

In the latter part of the 1800s, cattlemen and the like herded their longhorns along this trail by the millions, especially in Texas. It was a time to crop the ears, brand the cows and then move them north across Indian territory into Kansas, thus the beginning of the legend of the American cowboy.

The cattle drives took to one of three trails during this time, through what is now Oklahoma; the important trail, in terms of Fort Worth anyway, was obviously the Chisholm Trail, *the* major route out of Texas for livestock.

Surprisingly, though, this trail was only used from 1867 to 1884, but it certainly gained a reputation and also proved to be a wealthy trail for many, since the large numbers of longhorn cattle driven north meant lots of money for a state that was still recovering from the Civil War. Young cowboys riding mustangs also had a hand in glamorizing both the Chisholm Trail and the life of a cowboy with a Texas flavor to the point that eventually the "cowboy" became a hero in our time.

While the Missouri and Kansas borders were not allowing Texas longhorns to pass due to a deadly Texas fever the cattle carried for a time, the East was in need of beef, and it was up to Texas to supply it. In 1867, Kansas Pacific officials allowed for a small part of the land in Abilene, Kansas, for the Texas cattle to be brought through. That year alone, as many as 35,000 head came through, upping the following year; finally, in 1871, there was as many as 600,000 head of cattle that came through the trail.

The first Texas herd to follow the Chisholm Trail was the cattle of a man named O.W. Wheeler, who brought 2,400 steers from San Antonio and was planning to winter in the plains and head to California. However, after finding the wagon tracks that were actually made by Jesse Chisholm, he followed that trail instead, and soon after the Texas cowboys had given the trail its reputation.

Herds took to the Shawnee Trail by way of San Antonio, Austin, and Waco, but it was always the good old Chisholm Trail from Fort Worth that then passed by Decatur to the Red River Station that kept the city in business. From Fort Worth, the trail went north to Newton, Kansas, and these days U.S. Highway 81 follows the old Chisholm Trail.

By 1870, thousands of Texas longhorn cattle were being driven over the Chisholm Trail to the Union Pacific Railroad shipping center in Abilene, Kansas. By 1871, more than five thousand cowboys were being paid per day for their hard work, and while Fort Worth might have had a reputation in the South, there was one thing for sure: Fort Worth was never as rough as the town of Abilene.

The Chisholm Trail was closed with barbed wire by 1884 under the auspices of a Kansas quarantine law, but during its time, as many as 5 million cattle and 1 million mustangs had winded their way along the trail, many after leaving the city of Fort Worth.

Indeed, from the years 1866 to 1890, there were millions of heads of cattle that made the trip up the Chisholm Trail from Fort Worth, and that meant many cowboys stopping in Fort Worth along the way. Fort Worth's entertainment district was the talk of the trail for days, as was an area located just a few blocks from the courthouse: Hell's Half Acre.

In Hell's Half Acre, crime was rampant, and sections of town even became off-limits for the respectable folks living in Fort Worth. After all, with shootings, muggings and nightly brawls, no one was safe there.

Eventually, Hell's Half Acre, which began at the end of Rusk Street, now Commerce Street, spread to more than two acres by 1881, growing through four of the city's main north–south thoroughfares. It is also noted that Hell's Half Acre had been called during that time, specifically by 1876, the "Bloody Third Ward." It was at this time that City Marshal Jim Courtright decided to offer his protection, leading to his bloody end at the hands of the owner of the White Elephant Saloon. But he did end some of the violence, often putting more than two dozen people in jail on weekend nights. It was here, too, that the bandits and outlaws hid out until, finally, the place was too rough even for the cowboys to enjoy. This meant that the businesses suffered, too, but it took quite a while for anything to actually be done about it since "the Acre" was making money for the city anyway and since it was a thrill for wayward visitors.

The end of Hell's Half Acre really came right after Courtright was killed and a local prostitute was found murdered weeks later—not the kind of reputation that Fort Worth wanted, money or not. Then, of course, Texas's first prohibition campaign also took hold, and the worst of Hell's Half Acre had ended by 1889.

When the railroad came through in the 1870s, the Chisholm Trail was still an important part of Fort Worth's history, but even more so the spot then became an important shipping area for livestock. To this end, the Union Stockyards were built and became operational in 1889.

While it might have been built, at first there was no money for the Stockyards to excel. It needed to not only buy cattle but also attract ranchers, but it didn't have the means until the company's president, Mike C. Hurley, lulled a wealthy Yankee from Boston to the area, hoping that he would invest. He did invest, convincing others of the importance of the area, including Bostonian Louville V. Niles, a meatpacker. In 1893, the Union Stockyards changed its name to the Fort Worth Stockyards Company.

An East Exchange Avenue scene, circa 1913. *Courtesy of the Stockyards Museum.*

Grand champion hogs, sired by Shamrock, 1911. *Courtesy of the Stockyards Museum.*

There was also the Fort Worth Stockyards Exchange at 100 block, East Exchange Street, now designated as a Texas historical landmark. It was the gateway to the Fort Worth Stockyards and was completed in 1910. Constructed by the Topeka Bridge & Land Company for the Fort Worth Stockyards Company, the columns are twenty-two feet high and thirteen feet in circumference, and the sign is thirty-six feet long and four feet high, still an important landmark today.

The Fort Worth Stockyards hog and sheep markets, at 140 East Exchange Street, and the Fort Worth Stockyards horse and mule barns, at 120 East Exchange Street, are also worth mentioning. With the hogs and sheep markets, particularly, early attempts by the Fort Worth Union Stockyards Corporation had been valiantly made since 1887 to persuade Texans to produce more hogs. The attempt was always unsuccessful, so in 1903 the Fort Worth Stockyards constructed new hog and sheep pens and launched a promotional campaign, which included cash, livestock prizes and a youth Pig Club program, to persuade ranchers to raise more hogs. It is noted that this program worked and that hogs processed at the Stockyards increased from 150,527 in 1903 to 1,062,021 in 1917. The number of sheep processed also increased from 1903 through the 1920s. Texas had become the largest producing state for both cattle and sheep by the mid-1930s, and during World War II, cattle, sheep and hog numbers at the Fort Worth Stockyards also increased.

The Fort Worth Stockyards Company's wooden horse and mule barns on the original site were destroyed in 1911 by a fire on opening day of the Feeders and Breeders Show, but the show continued as planned, and former president Theodore Roosevelt gave the opening address. The company then announced that it would get rid of the barns and replace them with concrete and steel fireproof buildings (construction was completed in 1912).

Meatpacking plants also became popular in the area at this time since it was profitable to keep the business in Fort Worth, more so than shipping the cattle elsewhere. Other companies that came in at the time to get some action included Armour & Company and Swift & Company; both built plants near the Stockyards.

Armour built on the northern site and Swift on the southern site (the site of the original Livestock Exchange and Hotel), and Swift & Company also ended up with another windfall when it found a large gravel pit on its property, used eventually to build both plants. So, by 1902, the Livestock Exchange Building, pens, barns and everything along with them was in full swing and ready to go.

After a while, the Livestock Exchange Building was being referred to as the "Wall Street of the West." With the Stockyards having everyone talking, the next step was to build an indoor facility, which still stands today as the Coliseum, a showcase that unbelievably took just eighty-eight days to build in 1907. The first show in the Coliseum was the Feeders and Breeders Show, and it also sounded off with the first indoor rodeo.

Horse-drawn Armour & Company wagon, 1910. *Courtesy of the Stockyards Museum.*

The Swift pork cut and trim department, 1934. *Courtesy of the Stockyards Museum.*

Aerial view of the Armour and Swift stockyards, 1950. *Courtesy of the Stockyards Museum.*

Even in 1911, and after two fires that killed quite a large number of livestock, it was all about rebuilding and, of course, improving the facility using nonflammable material.

A new town called Niles City had also emerged in the area, appropriately called "the richest little city in the world" with property values as high as $30 million. Fort Worth annexed the area in 1923.

In 1917, when World War I was raging, the Fort Worth Stockyards was the largest horse and mule market in the world, and the military purchased its animals from there—during the war years, the livestock sales grew to great proportions.

In World War II, the same thing happened again, with numbers detailing that the Fort Worth Stockyards processed 5,277,496 head of livestock, with 1944 being one of the largest production years of all time. Keeping those numbers steadily high, there was not a decline until the late 1960s, with sales of only 1,045,158 head, and then in 1986, with a low of 57,181 animals sold.

Thinking back, however, it's easy to see how it all started with the Chisolm Trail. Many reasons can be attributed to why, over the years, there has been a decline in the sale of cattle. It's not what you might expect, though, since the truth is that it was the trucking industry that put the railroad shipping into a harder financial crisis after World War II with a new way of moving and selling livestock. Could Fort Worth keep up?

Today folks can visit the Stockyards and still get a firsthand experience of the rodeo, the local auctions and even those longhorns being driven down the street twice a day. The Stockyards did eventually end up falling on bad times financially, however.

In 1976, the North Fort Worth Historical Society, which both Charlie and Sue McCafferty founded, was formed to make sure that Fort Worth's livestock heritage would not die, so important was its function in the city for so many years. The Fort Worth Stockyards National Historical District was also established in 1976, and in 1989 the North Fort Worth Historical

A commissioner on horseback in cattle pens, 1920s. *Courtesy of the Stockyards Museum.*

Society opened the Stockyards Museum in the historic Exchange Building, but weekly livestock auctions ceased years ago, unfortunately.

With so much to see and do in the Fort Worth Stockyards area these days, a first stop might be at the Visitor Information Center, but for food and entertainment head right on over to Billy Bob's, a Stockyards staple even today.

Stock Show Timeline

Here is a timeline culled from the Fort Worth Stock Show and Rodeo website (www.fwssr.com), showing the rich history of one of the institutions that made Fort Worth what it is today.

1907—The first admission charged is twenty-five cents. The Stock Show Association is formed. The first formal horse show directly connected to the Stock Show takes place. On October 4, a cornerstone is set for Northside Coliseum.

A longhorn and its handler wait for business, 2011. *Photo by Russell William Dandridge.*

1908—The Northside Coliseum, site of the annual cattle show, is billed as "the most opulent and dynamic livestock pavilion in the entire Western Hemisphere." The Coliseum features enormous skylights, patriotic flags and bunting and incandescent lights. The Northside Coliseum is completed as the show's headquarters in February. Samuel Burk Burnett, founder of the famous 6666 Ranch, becomes the show's president. The show opens under a new name: the National Feeders and Breeders Show.

1909—The grand champion barrow is a prime specimen at the National Feeders and Breeders Show in north Fort Worth. The event later becomes known as the Fat Stock Show and is today called the Southwestern Exposition and Livestock Show. For the first time, the show runs concurrently with the Texas Cattle Raisers Association Meeting. On March 15, a parade featuring almost forty Comanche and Kiowa braves is led by Chief Quanah Parker. March 19 is the first and last time that prize show bulls are featured in parade.

1910—Going to the horse show is a "fashion statement." Shown here are the latest fashions of the day: high-crowned wide-brimmed felt hats, high-heeled boots and, for the ladies, split riding skirts. The first automobile exhibit opens at the Stock Show this year.

1911—Purebred cattle, such as the Hereford breed, are represented at the first exhibition in north Fort Worth. On March 14, Theodore Roosevelt, former president of the United States, is the guest of honor at the Stock Show.

1913—Baby Beef Clubs, the forerunners of 4-H Clubs, spring up around the country in the 1910s. The clubs aim to involve youngsters in educational programs, furthering the livestock industry. The first annual meeting is hosted in Fort Worth. The Stock Show's evening performance is opened by President Woodrow Wilson pushing a button in the White House, with the button "turning on" the electric lights of the Coliseum.

1916—The Miller Brothers 101 Ranch Wild West Show, held in the Coliseum during Stock Show, features performers Zach and Lucille Mulhall, whom Will Rogers named "the first cowgirl."

1918—The Stock Show adopts Southwestern Exposition and Fat Stock Show as its official name. When the rodeo is added to the Southwestern

Exposition and Fat Stock Show, crowds increase. Opening day of the rodeo is the unquestioned highlight of the year for thousands of people. The Northside Coliseum hosts the first indoor rodeo event as "strickly a contest"; events include ladies' bucking bronco, junior steer riding, men's steer riding and bucking bronco.

1920—Brahman bull riding is introduced to the Stock Show by rodeo producer Verne Elliott.

1922—Marion Samson Sr. becomes the Stock Show's president.

1923—Van Zandt Jarvis becomes the Stock Show's president; he serves for seventeen years, until his death in 1940.

1927—Side-release bucking chutes are introduced by Verne Elliott, producer of the Stock Show's rodeo. Bareback bronc riding is added to rodeo events.

1932—The first live radio broadcast of a rodeo on the National Broadcasting Company network takes place through Amon Carter's Fort Worth affiliate WBAP ("We Bring a Program").

1938—Turtles, a cowboy association, establishes an official list of rodeo events in January: bareback riding, calf roping, saddle bronco riding, bulldogging and steer (or bull) riding.

1940—John C. Burns becomes the Stock Show's president.

1943—There is no Stock Show held, due to World War II.

1944—The Stock Show moves to Will Rogers Memorial Center. Gene Autry becomes the first entertainer to appear at a rodeo.

1945—The Rodeo Cowboys Association national offices open in Sinclair Building in downtown Fort Worth.

1946—The Stock Show celebrated its golden (fiftieth) anniversary. The show had moved from the Northside to the west side of Fort Worth, the current site of the Will Rogers Memorial Complex, in 1944. As the livestock barns were not built, the cattle were sheltered in brightly colored tents.

1947—The Will Rogers *Riding into the Sunset* bronze statue, created by Electra Waggoner Biggs through a commission from Amon G. Carter Sr., is dedicated in November. Amon G. Carter Sr. becomes the Stock Show's first chairman of the board.

1948—Comedians Hoyt Heffner, Hank Mills and John Lindsey "successfully" wrestle a steer. Cattle Barns Nos. 1, 2, 3 and 4 and the sheep and swine barns are opened.

1949—Barn No. 5 is opened to house horses for equestrian competitions during the Stock Show.

1956—Barn No. 6 is opened to house livestock exhibits during the Stock Show. James M. North Jr. becomes the Stock Show's chairman of the board.

1958—The Fort Worth rodeo becomes the first to receive complete live national television coverage. Guest stars Roy Rogers and Dale Evans are hosts on NBC-TV, with George "Gabby" Hayes and the Sons of the Pioneers. Amon G. Carter Jr. becomes the Stock Show's chairman of the board.

1959—Connie Swinford sells her grand champion steer to Amon Carter Jr.

1963—Barn No. 7 is opened to house livestock exhibits during the Stock Show.

1964—The Old Round Up Inn building, which will house Stock Show offices, is built.

1965—Special entertainment at the rodeo includes an unusual riding team of Zippy riding a Scottish sheepdog. The animals are owned and trained by Tom Lucia of Weatherford.

1972—Barn No. 8 is opened to house livestock exhibits during the Stock Show.

1977—W.R. Watt Jr. becomes the Stock Show's sixth president.

1983—John Justin becomes the Stock Show's chairman of the board.

1984—*Midnight*, a life-sized bronze statue of one of the most famous bucking broncos, created by Jack Bryant through a commission from Amon G. Carter Jr. in 1982, is dedicated to Carter. The Amon G. Carter Jr. Exhibits Hall is opened.

1987—The Stock Show adopts Southwestern Exposition and Livestock Show as official name.

1988—The Will Rogers Equestrian Center is opened.

1996—The Stock Show celebrates its centennial anniversary. The Charlie & Kit Moncrief Building is opened this year and includes the 1,100-seat W.R. Watt Arena. The bronze statue *John Justin and "Baby Blue"* is also erected this year, and the Stock Show has a record paid rodeo attendance of 152,989.

1999—The Will Rogers Memorial Center gets a new "front door," which is the 2,300-square-foot ticket office and Fort Worth Convention and Visitors Bureau information center.

2001—Ed Bass is named Stock Show's chairman of the board.

2002—The Stock Show expands its schedule to twenty-three days and features its new Ranching Heritage Weekend. A record 951,000 visitors attend the show.

2004—Records were established with more than twenty-four thousand head of livestock entered and fourteen livestock sales that together generated $4,322,675.

2005—The Moos brothers, the official Fort Worth Stock Show ambassadors, help to spread the word that the Stock Show is the place to enjoy plenty of fun and family entertainment. From the educational exhibits to the livestock barns or the ever-popular midway rides, there's something for everyone. Easily identified by their attire, Hoss Moos insists on a cowboy hat, while Elwood Moos prefers a gimme cap. These Tarrant County natives are fun-loving bulls that will devote their lives to promoting the Stock Show.

2006—Stock Show added the sport of team roping to the PRCA event lineup. It will be held off-site until accommodations can be made in the Coliseum for the 2007 Stock Show.

2008—The Fort Worth Stock Show and Rodeo are inducted into the Pro Rodeo Hall of Fame.

2010—Upon the retirement of W.R. Watt Jr., Bradford S. Barnes is named president and general manager.

2011—This year is the twenty-fifth anniversary of the Fort Worth Calf Scramble.

THE FORT WORTH HERD

Longhorns were the best cattle for long drives in the early West since these animals have a natural ability to travel long distances, swim rivers and live through the hot summer sun and cold winters. Cowhands on the long cattle drives were known as "drovers," because they "drove" cattle. It was in 1999 that the twice-daily cattle drives began in the historic Stockyards. When they aren't taking their walk through town, the cattle are penned in the Stockyards so that visitors can see them there, too.

You can still see longhorn cattle in the Fort Worth Stockyards, just like in the 1800s, in this 2011 image. *Photo by Russell William Dandridge.*

Lodging in the Stockyards: Then and Now

Miss Molly's Bed & Breakfast
109½ West Exchange Avenue
Fort Worth, Texas
817-626-1522

Fort Worth's past comes alive at Miss Molly's hotel, a bed-and-breakfast in the heart of the historic Fort Worth Stockyards. Walking through the seven bedrooms is like spending time in a museum, and all have turn-of-the-century decor and antiques. Every room reflects parts of Fort Worth's colorful history. Some rooms feature cowboy and rodeo themes, while others capture the oil and railroad days.

Stonehouse Bed & Breakfast
2401 Elllis Avenue
Fort Worth, Texas
817-626-2589

Fort Worth's authentic "cowboy bed-and-breakfast," with eight detailed theme rooms. The property was an original cowboy boardinghouse used by local and out-of-town cowboys tending livestock in the nearby Fort Worth Stockyards. The building has the original wooden floors, walls and solid doors from a nearby 1800s building.

Stockyards Hotel
109 East Exchange Avenue
Fort Worth, Texas
1-800-423-8471
www.stockyardshotel.com

The Stockyards Hotel dates back to the turn of the century. It was in 1904 when one of North Fort Worth's early developers and entrepreneurs, Colonel T.M. Thannisch, purchased the property where he built the two-story frame building on the corner of North Main and East Exchange. With balconies on the western and southern sides, it was also home to the Stockyards Club Saloon and billiards parlor in the western portion, as well as furnished rooms for rent on the second floor. Businesses in the building at the time had their front doors situated on the southwest corner, which faced the intersection of Main and Exchange. Throughout the building's history, there have been an assortment of shops, including a barbershop, a confectionery shop, real estate and insurance offices and a restaurant in the eastern part of the building. In December 1906, Colonel Thannisch also began to build a three-story brick building on the far eastern part of the property, and this was for the hotel that still exists today. Finished in 1907, not just the hotel but also a restaurant, physicians' offices and the Club Saloon were located in this building, with everything at street level other than the hotel rooms.

Stuffed longhorns hung on the wall inside the Stockyards Hotel, 2011. *Photo by Russell William Dandridge.*

It was expanded in 1913 with a brick addition of three stories, with a basement. At this time, the hotel was also improved with the addition of community baths on each floor and ceiling fans in each room, as well as heat in the winter from the steam boilers in the basement.

The property was bought in 1982 and restored, finally opening again in 1984 as the Stockyards Hotel. In 1996, it was bought again by local investors. With fifty-two suites and sleeping rooms, the hotel is decorated in a variety of period styles with a turn-of-the-century flavor. There is also a restaurant and bar, adding to the atmosphere of the Old West. Is there also maybe a ghost? Some say yes.

Chapter 4

FORT WORTH IN THE EARLY
TO LATE 1900S

B y the time Fort Worth made it into the 1900s, it was a little town with a lot going for it and a bright future ahead. It was in 1902 that the Swift & Company, Armour & Company and McNeill & Libby packinghouses all landed in Fort Worth to make fortunes, and by the 1900s most of the dance halls and gamblers were a thing of the past, giving the city a bit more respectability. In place of the dance halls and gambling areas, there were cheap variety shows, and there was also some prostitution to keep the folks entertained. Places likes Hell's Half Acre were quickly being reformed around this time, too.

With so much to look at and be proud of from the earlier century—for example, the arrival of that first train and the Chisholm Trail cowboys—Fort Worth by the 1900s was Texas's fifth-largest town, and the next move was to work to make a name in regard to the packinghouses, right in the heart of the Southwest. With these packinghouses also came employment to the city for thousands of people. In fact, in 1910, when a census figure was taken, it reported that there had been a 76,312 increase in work in Fort Worth. Originally, the packinghouses were only for hogs. A second company, a refrigerating plant where beef was shipped, quickly failed, but when the board of trade took control, the meatpacking industry finally saw success with the help of the Fort Worth Dressed Meat and Provision Company, with stock of $500,000, enabling the Stockyards and the packing plant business to really begin.

However, even with the growth that the city was seeing, the streets were still dirty and sidewalks were made of wood. The tallest building was still only seven stories high. Of course the courthouse was impressive, since it

Right: Employees of the Swift Creamery, 1920. *Courtesy of the Stockyards Museum.*

Below: Thannisch Building Stockyards Club, Thannisch, proprietor, 1911. *Courtesy of the Stockyards Museum.*

had been finished, although many residents believed that the more than $400,000 that it cost to build had been too expensive.

By this time, Fort Worth had its share of modern amenities, such as its streetcar leading to neighborhoods and businesses, a university that had been chartered in the late 1800s, Texas Wesleyan University, and also Polytechnic University.

Still keeping its cattleman persona, the 1900s saw Fort Worth hosting the National Livestock Association's annual meeting, with more than four thousand stockmen from all over America descending on the city. A parade in conjunction with the event brought in as many as twenty thousand people, and the governor of Texas, Joseph D. Sayers, opened the convention to great success.

Also in the early 1900s, Buffalo Bill brought the Wild West to Fort Worth by opening his show, with more than ten thousand people in attendance to watch the stunts.

It didn't take the city long to build up its downtown area, either, and within ten years, one could hardly recognize the changes it had undergone. Eventually, horses and carriages gave way to automobiles, and dirt roads became cobblestone streets, the first block being on Sixth Street between Main and Houston. Additionally, every part of the city was open for new businesses and homes. The downtown area already had the Carnegie Library, built in 1901, as well as Greenwall's Opera House, the Vendome Theater and the Lyric, offering residents a taste of vaudeville. The first film, shown in 1903, was *The Great Train Robbery*.

Other important buildings that sprang up in Fort Worth in the first decade of the new century included the three-story Texas Lodge of the Knights of Pythias on Main Street, where meetings were held on the third floor; the Flatiron Building, considered the city's first skyscraper; a ten-story First National Bank Building; and many more as the years progressed. In 1909, the city's Fort Worth Gas Company was established with almost four thousand customers in the beginning, getting gas from a ninety-mile pipeline from Petrolia.

Also during the first decade, an area now a part of Fort Worth proper but then called Marine became an important part of the city, too, since it was located along the banks of the Trinity River. Marine was the area with most of the livestock and meatpacking ties, which meant money and trolley lines that ran through the area, with homes as diverse as mansions to one-room dwellings for workers.

This was also the area where today's Livestock Exchange Building is located, as well as the Coliseum and home to the National Breeders and Feeders Show, which was created to show off the district. Eventually changed to become the

The Livestock Exchange Building still remains in the Stockyards area today, 2011. *Photo by Russell William Dandridge.*

"Northside," the area included Rosen Heights, Diamond Hill and Washington Heights. There was also a lavish residential development built at that time called Quality Hill on the city's western bluff, and it was soon known as the place to live in Fort Worth, with amazing Trinity River views and the ability to see the distant plains and feel the inviting breezes "out west."

Other areas also grew up in the city, and some were not as lavish as the aforementioned developments. The regular guy lived and worked in communities like Brooklyn Heights, Glenwood and even the Garden of Eden, a small African America community south of Birdville on the Trinity River. Other areas that were building up fast included a spot south of downtown called the Fairmont addition, Prairie Chapel and residential areas near the universities.

During the 1910s, a large group of immigrants also made its way to Fort Worth and to the city's Northside. From Greeks to Bulgarians, Russians, Poles, Czechs, Spaniards and Mexicans, all descended on the bustling little town. The result was the transformation of the area (mainly near the Swift and Armour facilities), with each group bringing culture into the city in an effort to keep their old traditions alive. Many of the Europeans also saved up their money and were able to open stores or restaurants, making the city culturally diverse early on in its creation.

African Americans also found a place in Fort Worth, moving into the Lake Como area. A sale after a huge flood offered one dollar on land; by buying the land at the cut-rate prices, it was a steal. Also at this time, due to the migration, the Industrial and Mechanical College and the Union Church were established.

Religion also had a big hand in Fort Worth by this time, and one reverend at the First Baptist Church named J. Frank Norris decided to fight against racetrack gambling in 1911, as well as work to rid the city of prostitution. Things got dirty quick when Norris started pointing fingers at Hell's Half Acre and associating the place with some of the city's more prominent leaders. In 1912, after causing too much trouble, there was an attempt to burn down his church, a failed attempt the first time; a month later, though, the building did burn to the ground.

To make matters worse, Norris was then charged with the arson himself after a local milkman said that he had seen Norris running from the church building as the church was being engulfed with flames. Norris's attorney said no way, but there was a piece of paper that had been pulled from Norris's pocket that apparently still pointed the finger in his direction. The judge eventually found Norris not guilty. When the verdict came down, those in the courtroom rooting for the reverend broke into religious song. Even being acquitted, however, Norris still continued to attack the folks frequenting Hell's Half Acre. Finally, in 1917, with a new city administration and the federal government's help for its own purposes (to bring in a site for a military training camp), the Acre was a thing of the past. As it turned out, the local police department noted that at least 50 percent of the violent crime in Fort Worth had taken place in Hell's Half Acre over the years.

Amusement parks were excellent pastimes for the locals during the 1900s, with places like Lake Erie, Hurst Lake, White City and Lake Como quite popular. Rowboats, roller coasters, dancing, music and fireworks were the pleasures of the day, and at this time many Europeans had moved to the area, adding pieces of their culture to the mix. Today's Hermann Park grew out of a German biergarten and is linked to the German Society.

Of course, baseball and Texas had grown up together, and that was no different in Fort Worth, where the first baseball team, the Panthers, was established in 1877. In the 1900s, the New York Giants, Detroit Tigers and St. Louis Browns came through Fort Worth for exhibition season.

Local traditions that are still in place today also began back in the early 1900s, when the Fort Worth Fair and the Flower Parade and Festival began.

One very big thrill for Fort Worth was when, in 1905, President Teddy Roosevelt came through on his way to Oklahoma for a wolf hunt with local ranchers. He stopped in Fort Worth long enough to give a speech, much to the excitement of the locals living in the city.

By the time the first decade of the 1900s ended in Fort Worth, there was much to be proud of. Just as it had begun, the city was once again planning for another gathering of cattlemen to host twice the number of folks who had attended the first show in 1900.

Oil was discovered in 1917 in west Texas and had a big impact on Fort Worth since the farm where it was found was only about ninety miles west of the city. With World War I, the country needed more fuel, and this helped meet the demand, which was very good for the city. By the 1920s, five refineries had been built, and Fort Worth was an oil center, with a number of rich ranchers and farmers moving to town to build bigger homes and spend their money.

When World War I broke out in 1914, there were three flying fields built near the city and used by the United States government. With these three flying fields, Fort Worth had just acquired another industry: aviation. As many as seven thousand workers took part in building Taliaferro 1, 2 and 3, and by the time World War II began, the city was ready, with B-24 bombers being manufactured at a plant in Fort Worth.

Camp Taliaferro was a World War I flight training center run by the U.S. Army Signal Corps in the Fort Worth area. It was named after Walter R. Taliaferro, a U.S. Army aviator, and it offered facilities for members of the Royal Flying Corps (RFC) and U.S. forces from October 1917 to November 1918. The camp included airfields at Saginaw (Hicks Field), Benbrook (Carruthers Field) and Everman (Barron Field). During the winter of 1917, the RFC instructors trained about 6,000 men at this camp, and in six months, it is noted that up to 1,960 pilots were trained, completing sixty-seven thousand flying hours on the Curtiss JN4 Canuck, a two-seater biplane with speeds of about seventy-five miles per hour.

Bomber pilots also trained at what is now called Carswell Air Force Base. Camp Bowie was built in 1917 with as many as five thousand workers constructing 1,500 buildings on 1,410 acres. It was where the Thirty-sixth Division trained. Overall, the military payroll there was $1,675,000 per month.

In fact, government officials in the city worked hard to bring in the various companies related to the war since it meant a better economy. Camp Bowie was actually named after the co-commander of Alamo fame, James Bowie, in honor of the current selection of the camp in Fort Worth.

Fort Worth received the green light for the three aviation sites by beating out Dallas, Midland, Waco, Austin and Wichita Falls. The training fields were a big coup for the city since they meant big bucks, nearly $2 million alone in army payroll, and of course that also meant money being spent in the city. Continuing its move into aviation long into the future, one must not forget that when the Dallas/Fort Worth International Airport opened in 1974, it was the largest airport in the world. At one point in the 1900s, Fort Worth also had to deal with a more dire problem right at home: the Spanish influenza, which caused great fear in the city for a time. There was even a shortage of beds, blankets and hospital rooms for those who needed treatment. One example serves: an orphan came down with influenza but was turned away from the hospital and thus had to go back to the orphanage, infecting as many as one-quarter of the children living there. As quickly as the influenza had come, however, it was gone when the winter months took hold of the city.

The years between the two world wars were also an important time for Fort Worth, as it continued to see growth of every kind, with some of the architecture from that period still remaining today.

While there had been a free public school for years, it didn't take long for a boom to occur, with more schools and several historic buildings coming in; office buildings and the Texas, Worth and Blackstone Hotels also made huge impacts on the city. The railway station was commissioned, as was the terminal warehouse, the U.S. Courthouse and the U.S. Post Office, these being built on the south side of downtown during the second decade of the century.

By the last days of the decade, from 1910 to 1919, word was that the city was not building fast enough to keep up with the progress, something by this time that the residents of Fort Worth were demanding.

By the late 1930s, as much as $11 million was being spent on construction, which included the Will Rogers Memorial Coliseum and Auditorium, City-County Hospital, Public Health Service Hospital and a new city hall.

Fort Worth hit the ground running in the Roaring Twenties and didn't stop. From west Texas, more money just kept pouring in, with the vast amount of resources keeping Fort Worth on fire with industries from cotton to gin, oil and gas.

A larger-than-life character from Fort Worth, Amon Carter was the publisher of the *Fort Worth Star Telegram* and still remains a big piece of Fort Worth history throughout the 1900s but particularly during the Roaring Twenties. Not a caricature, Carter was definitely what folks think of when they think of a real "Texan." It is noted that he always wore a Stetson hat, with a bandana around his neck held in place by a diamond stickpin. He stuffed his well-tailored pants into his purple-and-white cowboy boots (now the colors of TCU), and he sometimes even wore chaps, spurs and a holster holding two pearl-handled pistols. A charmer for sure, Carter was bigger than life, and by the early 1920s his newspaper was already one of the largest in the southern states. Again, Carter made this decade of Fort Worth's history worth remembering in so many ways, making and keeping his connections usually at a club in Fort Worth or entertaining at Shady Oak Farms on Lake Worth.

It was also during this decade that the city was able to take a good look at its past and be proud of how far it had come. This resulted in 1923 with what was called a Diamond Jubilee held in commemoration. It was a weeklong affair, with parades and pageantry like never before seen in Fort Worth. It was billed as "the biggest the state had ever seen." There was also a film shown of Fort Worth in earlier times, as well as football games played, Indian war dances and, of course, an opening ceremony specifically created to remind folks of the city's stockyards roots, with a chuck wagon leading the way.

The mayor also requested that during the pageantry all of the folks of the city dress from the era from fifty to seventy-five years ago. Needless to say, residents loved it. With cowboys and pioneer costumes everywhere, each street in Fort Worth had a different theme and party, from jazz or orchestra to minstrels, snake charmers and fortunetellers. It was a different activity on each block below Main Street for folks to enjoy. The big event for the Diamond Jubilee that year was definitely the history pageant, with actors re-creating the military post establishment, the county seat being named in Fort Worth, the coming of the railway and even the Camp Bowie success.

Also during the 1920s, there was a boom of oil frauds who took money from innocent people, but even that scandal did little to prevent the oil drilling from continuing legitimately in the area. New buildings were also being added to the Fort Worth skyline, and the company Universal Mills came south during this decade, offering Fort Worth a chance to boast that it was the now the grain hub of the Southwest. Other businesses also moved south in the mid-1920s, with plants producing batteries, rubber products, bricks, boxes and even a variety of tools. Justin Boot Company moved to Fort Worth in 1925 and fit right in with the Stockyards and "Cowtown" image.

In 1922, railroad workers went on strike, but even worse was a meatpackers' strike that eventually resulted in violence, as could most strikes. It was a dark part of the city's history, and men were beat up and killed for crossing the picket lines.

As a cultural city by nature, in 1936 the world-famous Fort Worth Casa Mañana was built, being tagged the "House of Tomorrow." It was

Star Telegram owner Carter who fashioned the outdoor amphitheater and restaurant with a rotating stage and moat. Torn down due to the next world war, Casa Mañana made its comeback in 1958 and was rebuilt and remodeled again in the early 2000s. It is still standing today.

Another important addition to Fort Worth during the 1900s was the building of Lake Worth in the northwest part of the city. Finished in 1916, it cost about $1 million. While many folks don't remember this part of history, at one time there was an amusement-lined boardwalk on the lake, eventually being bypassed by the $6 million construction of Bridgeport and Eagle Mountain Lakes on the West Fork of the Trinity.

Boasting as many as thirty thousand people on holidays, Lake Worth had a roller coaster along the shoreline and an excursion boat in the lake that could carry as many as six hundred passengers, and it is noted that by the 1920s people were paying more and more money for entertainment, making the likes of the amusement parks and movie houses quite popular. Another plus for entertainment venue attendees was that most of the places had air conditioning by this time, and because of the often brutally hot Texas summers, people flocked to these places just to stay cool.

At the end of the 1920s, one thing did happen that affected the country, even though at first it almost went unnoticed in Fort Worth, as it was only a dim problem in the city: the stock market crash of 1929. In fact, in the beginning, the paper reported the crash as a number two story behind a more local robbery. A few days later, the crash wasn't even reported on the front page.

In the 1930s, the crash did eventually affect the city since unemployed workers were coming in by the multitudes, and the collapse in stock prices meant problems with economic ties in the other part of the country. With Fort Worth still in business—in fact, Fort Worth led the way in building among cities in Texas in 1929 and 1930—people were pouring in for jobs and bringing fresh waves of transients in daily looking for work, especially in construction. The city opened its arms and did its best to take care of and feed the influx of people.

Also during this time, there were no shortages of bank robberies. One robbery in Fort Worth that was especially memorable was that of a heist that had to do with a United States mail truck. While the heist ended up being a double crossing in the end, and a murder resulted, it brought to light the likes of O.D. Stevens, the head of a crime operation in the city and in the Southwest. Narcotics and bootlegging were on his list of crimes, but in 1933 he and some of his associates held up a mailroom at the railway station. With $72,000, he headed to New York to launder the money out of state. When he returned to Fort Worth, several of his associates met with him and demanded their share of the money, but both men were killed at point-blank range. With a few of Stevens's other associates helping, they got rid of the bodies the good old way: with concrete, dumping the bodies into the Trinity River. The dead men's wives, however, began to look for their husbands, and a young boy actually saw the bundle of concrete and dead flesh floating on the Trinity River surface before sinking. He reported it accordingly. Following a trial, Stevens was sentenced to the electric chair along with one of his associates, and the others involved were sentenced to many years in prison. Stevens somehow managed to escape the electric chair after a reversal and ended up only spending sixteen years in prison.

Other outlaws who came through Fort Worth in the 1930s included Machine Gun George Kelly; in fact, he even lived at his mother-in-law's house for a time in the city. Bonnie and Clyde enjoyed time in Fort Worth, too.

In 1933, prohibition ended, and it didn't take Fort Worth long to learn to enjoy a drink. The then assistant city manager opened the first legal beer that day, and by the end of the day, Fort Worth citizens had drank roughly thirty thousand cases and 12,800 drinks from the tap to celebrate the end of prohibition.

The 1930s also brought spending on even more entertainment, such as the aforementioned Casa Mañana, but other places, too, easily put Fort Worth on the map, such as the Will Rogers Memorial Center. Billboards around town read "Fort Worth for Entertainment; Dallas for Education." Then, an idea for what was called a frontier centennial became a reality with locals—a four-month run of Broadway musicals, sideshows, a frontier village and even freak shows; nothing was off-limits in regards to entertainment, and it was also during this celebration that Casa Mañana made its debut.

Losing almost $100,000 on the event, Fort Worth didn't mind since the show brought the city millions of visitors who now knew the city well. One thing that did not materialize in time for the show—which was a great disappointment since it had been billed as the show's highlight—was the Will Rogers Memorial Center. Around this time, too, the Botanical Gardens, still thriving in Fort Worth today, was established. A federal relief project, with an eye toward a European park design, the Botanical Gardens and many of the current Fort Worth landmarks were built around a thriving city working hard not to become just another casualty of the Great Depression.

Fort Worth had a huge involvement in World War II during those years, with the home of a Quartermaster Depot, Marine Air Base and the Fort

Worth Army Air Field taking important roles during this time. There was also an aircraft plant built on the shore of Lake Worth. During the war, the plant produced more than three thousand B-24 Liberator bombers and employed thirty-two thousand locals. Changing hands over the years, the plant also saw the production of the B-36 Peacemaker and the F-16 Fighting Falcon.

In the 1940s, at the Tarrant Field Airdrome, as many as four thousand World War II pilots got their wings, and Carswell Air Force Base was named in 1948 after a local hero of the same name put Carswell on the map. The base (through the courage of some of its pilots) also won a Distinguished Service Cross in 1944 after the successful sinking of a Japanese cruiser and a destroyer.

At this time, sure the city was focused on the war, but there was also an entertainment aspect. For example, the city featured the show *The Westerner* starring Gary Cooper, and Cooper came to Fort Worth and participated in a parade that drew hundreds of spectators, with him signing autographs for everyone. Also in this decade, Fort Worth clubs had the likes of Louis Armstrong, Cab Calloway and Sarah Vaughn perform, specifically at the Jim Hotel, despite the mixed audience. By now, much of Fort Worth had forgotten about this aspect anyway, since to locals it was much more important to hear jazz and blues at its best.

Like every other city during the war, Fort Worth had its share of rationing. For women, Rosie the Riveter really did exist in Fort Worth, where at the Convair plant there was a gender-equal mentality during the war years. By the time the war was over and the troops began to return, Fort Worth had changed. The population had escalated, with a mere sixty-five square miles of the city having ballooned to more than one hundred square miles. The cities surrounding Fort Worth weren't exactly eager to join up with Fort Worth, however, in order to avoid the high taxes, but those surrounding towns were certainly in a growth pattern at this time.

Another event of particular notoriety to Fort Worth and Carswell Air Force Base happened in the 1940s: the Roswell incident. Local air force personnel sent the debris from the Roswell site to Fort Worth's Carswell, where authorities assured locals and the world that the wreckage was only of a high-altitude balloon. Still a mystery today, many wondered what happened to the "aliens" that were being called anthropomorphic test dummies, but nothing has ever been determined either way.

In 1944, the Fat Stock Show started up again, this time being held at the Will Rogers Coliseum. A parade, which Fort Worth residents always loved, was also held. In the end, a large crowd of thirty-two thousand attendees showed up for the Fat Stock Show.

From the 1950s on, Fort Worth just kept growing, making a name for itself. With its postwar prosperity, Fort Worth continued to take on a number of different faces. With the air force putting the city in the national spotlight, new buildings were also being built during this time, like the thirty-one-floor Continental National Bank in 1956, with a very unusual revolving clock erected at the top of the building being most noticeable.

Another big achievement for Fort Worth in the 1950s was the announcement that Bell Aircraft Corporation was coming to town. To take on fifty-five acres, the company was expected to be a multimillion-dollar helicopter factory, with government contracts that again were destined to bring new business into the area. When all was said and done, the company hired 3,500 employees and made turbine-powered HU-1s, as well as a variety of other models.

Other noteworthy attractions are mentionable as the years went by in the 1950s, from Elvis Presley coming to town in 1956 and playing a packed Northside Coliseum to a decade that was ready and waiting for the crazy 1960s.

The Vietnam War and the Kennedy assassination, as well as many of the major events in the 1960s, left Fort Worth as stunned as the rest of the country. Also in the 1960s, the area known as Arlington became the entertainment mecca for Dallas and Fort Worth. Offering Fort Worth residents what they loved—more amusement parks—the main attraction became Six Flags Over Texas. Opening in 1961, more than fifteen thousand attended the opening of Six Flags Over Texas, and today the park is still hosting guests from around the world. Now, too, more than ever in fact, the city is still moving into the future, an emergence that began in the early part of the 1900s and is going strong today.

As for the remnants of the history that was such an important part of the 1900s for Fort Worth, much is still available to be seen throughout the city, with some of the major companies from that time still in existence.

THE 1900S AND THE IMPORTANCE JUST OUTSIDE THE CITY LIMITS

One of the most important events in the history of Fort Worth actually happened outside of Fort Worth in a town called Ranger, Texas, ninety miles away. Ranger was a one-horse town on the railroad line for most of its life. There was oil in the area, however, and while some folks didn't believe, the ones who did have the foresight got rich quick when oil was discovered in 1917. In fact, Ranger was transformed into an oil town not soon forgotten, putting itself and surrounding cities like Fort Worth on the map. Discovery of oil in Desdemona, south of Ranger, and Breckenridge, thirty miles northwest of Ranger, was a big deal. By this time, Texas was receiving national attention, specifically Fort Worth, with its significant role in the oil boom. Fort Worth's proximity in between the two booming areas and the fact that it was a metropolis meant that folks could enjoy the big city, which was a good place to spend all that oil money.

Banking, of course, became big business in Fort Worth, with the city playing a significant role for the group of oilmen pouring into the city with pockets full of money, ready to spend it on real estate or any other form of entertainment they desired.

Fort Worth also had three oil refineries early on, and five more were built by 1920, with more in the works. In fact, the refineries and the network of lines in the area gave Fort Worth the distinction of being called "the pipeline center of Texas."

Mexico and the Hispanic population that migrated to the area have also had a longtime claim to the city of Fort Worth. After all, since the founder of the fort there was a Mexican-American war hero, perhaps this is appropriate, and the city has certainly played a significant role in regard to Mexico ever since.

During the early years, what were known as barrios began to emerge around the local packing plants and, with them, the Hispanics who had moved to the area as early as the 1800s, into what was called "Lower Calhoun," located between Hell's Half Acre and the Stockyards at that time. Other Hispanic areas were built up as well, with most of the immigrants from Mexico working as laborers or domestic help but also opening grocery stores, bars and barbershops. Most of the Hispanics who did come to Fort Worth in the early part of the last century can trace their immigration to roughly 1910, during the Mexican civil war of that time. However, not long after that, America had a war of its own to worry about.

Preservation

A constant reminder of history and the importance it plays on a city can often be seen through the buildings that remain as a city grows and prospers. An organization called Historic Fort Worth was established in 1969 as a nonprofit charitable organization with an eye toward ensuring that history is preserved in the city. Since 2003, the organization has made a list of endangered places in Fort Worth. Of particular note are the single-screen

The New Isis Theater, 1940. *Courtesy of the Stockyards Museum.*

theaters in the city, with two having already been demolished and three being on the endangered list, including the 1935 New Isis Theater on North Main.

This past year, the organization was also concerned about the bluffs above the Trinity River. Those bluffs are in memory of General William Jenkins Worth, from when Fort Worth was established on June 6, 1849, by Major Ripley A. Arnold on the bluffs overlooking the confluence of the West and Clear Forks of the Trinity River. The bluffs are also part of the Chisholm/Eastern Trail that identifies Fort Worth as "Cowtown," and the location was also vital in establishing the location of the Tarrant County Courthouse.

Farrington Field (built from 1938 to 1939 and designed by Preston M. Geren in a classical modern style), Fort Worth Power & Light Company/ TXU Plant, the Hazel Harvey Peace House, the residence at 760 Samuels Avenue, a late nineteenth-century Getzendanner House and the Texas & Pacific Warehouse are also on the list of possible historical casualties, but with a city focus to preserve the old, much of Fort Worth's history, it seems, will not be lost in time.

Chapter 5

SIGNIFICANT PEOPLE AND TALL TALES

With many names associated with Fort Worth from one time to another, there are definitely a few folks from the city who will never be forgotten. After all, at this point the city, county and the surrounding areas have certainly etched the names of these people into the annals of history.

For example, the name General William J. Worth, for whom the town was named, will always live on in history. Worth not only has the city of Fort Worth named after him but also Lake Worth, Texas; the village of Worth, Illinois; Worth County, Georgia; the Lake Worth Lagoon in Florida; and the city of Lake Worth, Florida—all named in his honor.

When the Mexican-American War began, Worth was serving in Texas, and he was the one who actually negotiated the surrender of the Mexican city of Matamoros. He commanded a number of divisions and over time became a war hero not to be forgotten. When U.S. forces entered Mexico City in the 1800s, Worth personally climbed to the roof of the National Palace and took down the Mexican flag, replacing it with the Stars and Stripes. For his service at the Battle of Chapultepec, the United States Congress awarded him with a sword of honor. Worth died of cholera in 1849 in San Antonio.

Other recognizable names are also associated with the city of Fort Worth in one way or another. For example, Fort Worth itself is located in Tarrant, Parker Denton and Wise Counties, but Tarrant comes from General Edward H. Tarrant, one of the men who negotiated the local peace treaty when meeting with the local Native American chiefs.

Another county nearby, Van Zandt County, was named after Major K.M. van Zandt, who had a huge part in bringing the T&P Railroad into Fort Worth.

NAMES OF SIGNIFICANCE

Amon G. Carter (1879–1955), who was a civic booster and philanthropist, was also the creator and publisher of the *Fort Worth Star Telegram*. Born in Wise County, Texas, on December 11, Amon Giles Carter left home early and worked at a number of jobs around the country before he ended up in Fort Worth in 1905.

Today it is reported that the *Fort Worth Star Telegram* is among the top fifty papers circulated in the United States. It was in 1905 when Carter took a job as an advertising space salesman in Fort Worth, and a few years later, he decided to help finance and run the *Fort Worth Star* paper. They published the first paper in 1906, and after ups and down Carter thought that it would be a good idea to purchase the paper's competition, the *Fort Worth Telegram*. That happened in 1908, and in 1909 the paper's official named was changed to the *Fort Worth Star Telegram*.

There was also another paper in Fort Worth during that time, from 1900 to 1975, called the *Fort Worth Press*, a daily published in the afternoons. That paper was owned by the E.W. Scripps Company, but the *Fort Worth Star Telegram*, Carter's baby, outlasted everything.

Carter's involvement in many things relating to Fort Worth left a mark on many Texas institutions. It was in 1921 that he green-lighted the purchase of equipment that resulted in the establishment of WBAP Radio in Fort Worth. He also loved aviation and is given credit for helping attract the industry to the area. He spent a lot of the money he made in oil on philanthropic interests (including the Amon Carter Museum as a gift to Fort Worth). Today Carter is buried in Greenwood Cemetery. He died in Fort Worth on June 23, 1955.

Another significant name from the Fort Worth history books is Fred Cotton. Cotton was the onetime president of the Texas State Historical Association, and he helped develop Fort Worth's Log Cabin Village after realizing the importance of maintaining the city's heritage.

Billy Muth (1902–1949) made quite a number of important contributions to Texas history after moving to Fort Worth in 1926. Muth was born in Allentown, Pennsylvania, and was a church organist beginning at the age of nine years old. Nationally known as the master of the keyboard, he was the organist at Casa Mañana during the 1936 Texas centennial, a Worth Theatre multi-instrument Fort Worth Symphony musician and a church organist. A Paramount/Publix Theaters' pipe organist, Muth opened in theaters across the United States and throughout his life performed concerts and benefits and taught statewide organ and music seminars.

Fort Worth native Euday Louis Bowman was a ragtime composer whom most folks know from the classic "Twelfth Street Rag" tune. Bowman wrote this song about his experiences in Kansas City, Kansas. While it was copyrighted in 1914, it didn't become a hit until much later, in 1948, when it was recorded by Walter "Pee Wee" Hunt. Bowman died of pneumonia in New York City in 1949 and is buried in Oakwood Cemetery in Fort Worth.

Born Canadian, Ephraim Merrill Daggett was raised in Indiana on a farm and moved to the republic of Texas in 1838. Early on, he learned to trade with the Indians while at Fort Dearborn in Chicago before moving to Texas. While there, he became involved in the east Texas Regulator-Moderator feud and served as a captain in the Mexican-American War of 1846. He served on the Texas state legislature from 1851 to 1853 and established a mercantile business and hotel in Fort Worth in the early 1850s. He also moved his family there and purchased large tracts of real estate. Daggett used his influence as a former legislator to help secure Fort Worth's selection as county seat in 1860, and he also served as a brigadier general during the Civil War and then got heavily involved in the mercantile and cattle business in Fort Worth. His likeness is on the city's first seal, and his role in bringing the Texas & Pacific Railroad to Fort Worth in 1876 is also remembered. He is often given credit for helping transform Fort Worth from an abandoned military post to a center of commerce. These days, he is still known as the "Father of Fort Worth," and he is buried in Pioneer's Cemetery in the city.

General H.P Mabry, originally from Georgia, came to Texas in 1851. He served on the Texas legislature from 1856 to 1860 and was also involved with a Confederate expedition that captured Forts Washita and Arbuckle in Indian territory in 1861. In June 1861, he helped win the Wilson's Creek battle, but after many such conflicts he ended up with his arm shattered in a fight that was started because he was accused of spying. He eventually settled down and practiced law in Fort Worth from 1879 to 1885.

Tall Tales

Of course, along with the colorful folks who have lived and died in Fort Worth, it's no wonder that there are a few good tales that go along with the city, too. As for legends and stories, they abound in Fort Worth, but if you ask around, there are a few that just become better in the retelling.

For example, one very popular legend that many folks swear is true is the legend that Miss Molly's Bed & Breakfast, located near the historical

Stockyards on West Exchange Avenue, is haunted. About a block west of the old Fort Worth Stockyards, the bed-and-breakfast is a vintage affair located upstairs above the Fort Worth's Star Café, with eight rooms touting old-time western themes like "Cowboys," "Miss Jolies" (a madam from the 1940s) or "Gunslinger." Reports say that there have been manifestations in all of the rooms at one time or another.

The ghostly children that have manifested are suspected to be the young ones who, before the age of vaccinations, perhaps died of typhoid, polio, smallpox, measles, whooping cough or diphtheria. Perhaps a few of the ghosts seen are women who lived in the house during an earlier time, à la prostitutes who were notoriously involved in scandalous affairs, even leading to a few suicides.

Noted by many, "Miss Molly's is considered one of the most haunted buildings in Fort Worth, and one of the most active paranormal sites in Texas."

In fact, according to stories, in addition to all the rooms having experienced paranormal occurrences, those in the private quarters have also experienced weird happenings, too, from full-bodied apparition appearances to missing items, unexplained shadows, noises and cold spots. Unexplained aromas of perfume are often reported in the rooms and the hallway, and guests and staff have reported the disappearances of belongings and items that will appear again later, sometimes in the same place and sometimes elsewhere.

Toilets also flush without prompting, lights turn off and on and unlocked doors are said to sometimes be blocked from opening by unseen forces.

There is also, reportedly, the entity of a young girl of eight or nine years who lived in the house during an earlier time and apparently died of a disease or accident. She has appeared to some folks in the private rooms. A reporter once woke up in the middle of the night and claimed to see the apparition of a blonde woman sitting on the edge of his bed. Whatever the case, the story is that owners, staff and guests have all experienced paranormal activity.

The history of the bed-and-breakfast actually goes back to the 1800s, during that wild time when the cowboys came through town on the way to drive their longhorns north. Miss Molly's actually began as a proper boardinghouse in 1910 called the Palace Rooms. Roughly fifteen years later, with prohibition, the house changed hands and was renamed to the Oasis, becoming a speakeasy for illegal drinking.

By the 1940s, the boardinghouse had become a bordello called the Gayatte Hotel, sexually servicing cowboys, others in town who were involved in the livestock business and pretty much any of the shadier crowd who had the desire to visit. When the Texas government finally stopped tolerating prostitution, the people at the bordello ended up in trouble. The building was put on the real estate market until new owners renovated the building, started the Fort Worth's Star Café on the ground floor and turned the upper stories into Miss Molly's Bed & Breakfast.

Even with the many legends at the bed-and-breakfast, it is hard to tell just who or what might be haunting Miss Molly's, but there have been a number of psychic investigations, including the Texas Christian University's paranormal activity class, which visits on a regular basis.

Miss Molly's website notes: "The entities who remain in this building apparently are not shy in making contact with the living, especially males. The owners of this haunted bed and breakfast have on display in the common living areas, copies of unusual photos, tape recordings of EVPs, and the results and conclusions of the various investigators, for all to read."

Apparently, various members of these paranormal groups are also said to have made contact with the entities, mostly prostitutes who lived in the house in the 1940s and 1950s. Many had been either murdered or died of disease.

The Shaw gristmill at Log Cabin Village. *Courtesy of the City of Fort Worth's Log Cabin Village.*

Another interesting Fort Worth ghost legend has to do with the tale of a ghost at Log Cabin Village. Called the Lilac Ghost, many folks have noted that the place feels eerie, as if you are stepping back in time to the 1800s. There are seven log cabins that were brought to the village from around the state dating from the 1840s to the 1860s. Originally homes for families long ago, one of the log cabins seems to have a particularly interesting history. Located near the Trinity River in the city's Forest Park area, by 1963 the log cabins at the village had all been restored; finally, in 1966, Log Cabin Village was opened.

The village is actually a living history museum, meaning folks who work there dress up like they lived back in the time and also spend time in the cabins dressed as various artisans, showing how things were done in the 1800s, from making candles to spinning thread. As the village became more popular over the years, another cabin was added in 1975, and it is actually in this cabin in which the legend of the Lilac Ghost began—there have been a number of strange encounters mentioned as happening there.

At one time, back in 1850, the home belonged to a man with a young son, as well as a nanny who was living with them by the name of Jane Holt. It is a two-story log cabin and also doubles as the visitor center and a store. Rumor is that Jane died in the cabin. One of the bedrooms upstairs is where many folks mention smelling the scent of lilac flowers, and some say that they have even seen her in the room—usually just a faint look and mostly out of the corner of the eye.

Other tall tales from the Fort Worth area include stories of wayward outlaws; however, it is a known fact that Bonnie and Clyde definitely came through these parts and stayed at the Stockyards Hotel. Both are actually buried in Dallas, and of course, most folks swear that Butch Cassidy and the Sundance Kid really spent some time in the Stockyards area.

Shine a Light

The world's second-longest-burning light bulb is located in Fort Worth and has been burning for one hundred years, with no sign of stopping. Stories confirm that this tall tale is true and that the light bulb is still working at the Stockyards Museum. First installed in September 1908 above a backstage door at the Byers Opera House on Seventh Street, the opera house later became the Palace Theatre, which was torn down in 1977. But the bulb lived on, and with records taken by the staff at the opera house back in the day, they knew of every bulb replacement and equipment change they made. The bulb is left on at all times these days, and even the folks at *Ripley's Believe It or Not!* have made note of it. After the Palace was torn down, the property owner took the bulb home and left it burning for another fourteen years, and then it ended up at the Stockyards Museum. It's still burning in a display case in the museum, though not quite as brightly anymore.

Famous Names and Deeds

The following is a list of names of many others who have either lived or still live in Fort Worth and/or made contributions to the city's history.

Adrienne Ames (1907–1947), actress.
B.W. Aston (1936–2010), historian.
Sid Bass (born 1943), Sundance Square developer and major stockholder in the Walt Disney Company.
Alan Bean (born 1932), astronaut.
Mel Bradford (born 1934), literary critic.
Betty Buckley (born 1947), actress.
T-Bone Burnett (born 1948), songwriter, record producer, musician and singer.
Joel Burns (born 1969), politician.
Mark David Chapman (born 1955), assassinated John Lennon.
Kelly Clarkson (born 1982), singer and *American Idol* winner.
Van Cliburn (born 1934), famous pianist.
Ornette Coleman (born 1930), jazz musician.
Bobby Day (1928–1990), musician.
Kirk Franklin (born 1970), famous gospel singer and producer.
Edna Gladney (1886–1961), founder of the Edna Gladney Home.
Kay Granger (born 1943), congresswoman and former mayor of Fort Worth.
Judy Graubart (born 1943), actress, *The Electric Company.*
Brad Hawpe (born 1979), Major League Baseball player for the Colorado Rockies.
Larry Hagman (born 1931), actor, son of actress Mary Martin.
Phil Handler (1908–68), National Football League football player and coach.
Julius Hemphill (1938–1995), jazz composer and saxophone player.
Ronald Shannon Jackson (born 1940), jazz drummer.
Yale Lary (born 1930), Football Hall of Famer.
Debra Lehrmann (born 1956), family court judge and Republican nominee for the Texas Supreme Court, Place 3, November 2, 2010.

Jeff Newman (born 1948), Major League Baseball all-star baseball player.

"Pappy" O'Daniel (1890–1969), governor of Texas, U.S. senator and radio personality.

Ashlee Nino (born 1985), dancer, drummer, fashion designer, model and actress.

Lee Harvey Oswald (1939–1963), accused assassin of President John F. Kennedy.

Bill Owens (born 1950), former governor of Colorado (1999–2007).

Bill Paxton (born 1955), actor, directed/starred in the movie *Frailty*.

Dewey Redman (1931–2006) African American free jazz saxophonist.

Sid W. Richardson (1891–1959), oilman, cattleman and philanthropist.

Rod Roddy (1937–2003), television announcer on *The Price Is Right*.

Johnny Rutherford (born 1938), race car driver.

Bob Schieffer (born 1937), journalist, *CBS Evening News* anchor and *Face the Nation* host.

Tom Schieffer (born 1947), U.S. ambassador to Japan, candidate for Texas governor.

Kelly Shoppach (born 1980), catcher for the Pawtucket Red Sox.

Liz Smith (born 1923), journalist.

Soapy Smith (1860–1898), infamous con man who started his career in Fort Worth.

Latham Staples (born 1977), civil rights activist and founder of the Empowering Spirits Foundation.

Townes van Zandt (1944–1997), country music singer-songwriter.

Daniel E. Walker (1927–2009), civil servant known for rescue of charred remains of an American flag burned in protest at the 1984 Republican National Convention in Dallas.

Lisa Whelchel (born 1963), actress, played in the TV sitcom *The Facts of Life*.

James C. Wright Jr. (born 1922), U.S. congressman from Texas and Speaker of the House.

Jeana Yeager (born 1952), aviator, broke distance records during her (and Dick Rutan's) nonstop flight around the world in the experimental Voyager airplane in 1986.

Chapter 6

OLD HOMES, BUILDINGS AND CEMETERIES

There are sixty-two sites in Fort Worth that are on the National Register of Historic Places. From churches to old homes, schools and even historic districts like the Central Hadley Historic District, Fairmount-Southside Historic District, Elizabeth Boulevard Historic District, the Masonic Widows and Orphans Home Historic District and the near southeast historic district, to name a few.

To that effect, there are many more buildings, schools, homes and even cemeteries in Fort Worth that have been designated on the Texas Historical Register. Indeed, the city of Fort Worth has long taken pride in its history, and that's why there are so many reminders today of the city's past, still available for the visitor and the local to enjoy.

St Patrick's Catholic Cathedral is the oldest continuously used church building in Fort Worth, dating from 1888, when the cornerstone was laid. Located downtown on Throckmorton south of Tenth Street, it stands in Gothic Revival style, with twin towers that flank the gabled nave. The towers were designed as the bases for spires, but those were never completed. However, there is a large rose window in the front above the main entrance. The other windows and entryways are pointed arches with leaded glass. Currently, the old building has a congregation of four thousand members and is listed as a Texas historic landmark.

Mount Gilead Baptist Church (1912–2003) was founded in 1875 and is the oldest African American Baptist church in Fort Worth. The Mount Gilead congregation had been in several other locations before this building was constructed at 600 Grove Street. It was designed by William

A. Rayfield, a black architect, and was built in a Neoclassical style. Its outstanding features are the front portico with six nonfluted columns, pediment gables and simple exterior moldings, which all define the Greek Revival architecture. There are also semicircular arched windows with a Romanesque style.

First Christian Church (1915–2003) was founded in 1855, making it the oldest continuously operating church establishment in Fort Worth. The present building at Sixth and Throckmorton was designed by architects E.W. van Slyke and Clyde Woodruff in a Renaissance Revival style. Its outstanding features are a copper-clad dome and three porticos with Corinthian columns. Despite a small congregation of four hundred and considerable pressures to move, the church has retained its historic building, which was designated as an official Texas historical landmark in 1970 and was listed on the National Register of Historic Places in 1983.

The Tarrant County Courthouse, since its completion in 1895, has been the focal point for millions of people traveling north on Main Street in downtown Fort Worth. The building was built at a cost of little more than $400,000. Even though it was built "under budget," the citizens of Fort Worth still voted all the county commissioners out of office at the next election for their extravagant spending—a depressed economy led to bitter frustration with the commissioners by the Fort Worth electorate.

Old Buildings Still Standing

Buildings often play as big a part in the history of a city as do the people who built the lasting structures. The Arlington Heights Lodge No. 1184, A.F. and A.M., still located on Camp Bowie Boulevard, was chartered on December 9, 1921, and can be found on land donated by Lodge members W.C. Stonestreet and F.H. Sparrow. This building, designed by Lodge member John C. Davies, was dedicated in January 1923. It's a Classical Revival structure with a Greek temple influence, including pediment gables, brick pilasters with stone capitals, round-arch upper windows and entry, stone motif details and art glass transoms.

Known in the early 1900s as the tallest building in north Texas, the Flatiron Building still on Houston Street was erected in 1907. Designed by firm of Sanguinet & Staats, distinguished Fort Worth architects, of reinforced concrete over steel frame, this Renaissance Revival structure was inspired by the wedge-shaped Flatiron Building in New York.

The Tarrant County Courthouse at Main and Weatherford Streets was designed by the firm of Gunn & Curtis and built by the Probst Construction Company of Chicago from 1893 to 1895. This red Texas granite building, in Renaissance Revival style actually looks much like the Texas State Capital with the exception of the clock tower.

Catholics in Fort Worth began meeting together for the first time in 1875 in private homes, with traveling priests stopping in the town when available. In 1876, Bishop Claude Dubuis of the diocese of Galveston assigned a young Irish priest, Father Thomas Loughrey, to establish a parish in Fort Worth. In July 1876, the diocese purchased two lots at this site for a church to be named for Polish Jesuit saint Stanislaus Kostka. Within three months, on October 29, 1876, Father Loughrey said the first High Mass in the frame structure. Today the site is marked as the Saint Stanislaus Kostka Catholic Church, on Throckmorton. Serving the church until 1884, when a new pastor came in, a school was opened, with classes being taught by the Sisters of Mercy after 1885. A new church was finished in 1892 to replace Saint Stanislaus Kostka—it was named for Saint Patrick. The original Saint Stanislaus building became part of the school, but it came down in 1908 to make way for a new parish rectory.

Old Homes Listed as Texas Historic Landmarks

Fort Worth has a long and interesting history, and some of that history has easily been preserved through the old homes that were built in the late 1800s and the early 1900s. Prominent residents moved to the area and created homes for themselves while also having the foresight to cherish the past while thinking of the city's future. Many of these old and preserved homes in Fort Worth are listed as Texas historic landmarks and are a reminder today of Fort Worth's rich history.

The Baldridge House (at 5100 Crestline Road) was originally part of the Chamberlain–Arlington Heights development of the 1890s. Earl and Florence Baldridge built the home in 1910–13, and it was designed by the architectural firm of Sanguinet & Staats. Limestone columns line the façade, and carved oak woodwork decorates the interior.

The Cobb-Burney House (at 1598 Sunset Terrace), located on the bluff of the Clear Fork of the Trinity River, was built in 1904 for mortgage company president Lyman D. Cobb and his wife, Emma. She sold the home in 1919 to a man in the cattle industry. Notice the low-pitched roof and the wide, overhanging eaves of the many casement windows that were obviously influenced by the Chicago Prairie School style of architecture.

The Dr. Clay Johnson House (at 3 Chase Court) was finished in 1912 and was designed by the Fort Worth architectural firm of Waller & Field. The Prairie School influence is also found here, with the horizontal roofline and broad cornices, but there are also classical details noted in the semicircular windows and the balustrade around the roof.

The Dr. George M. Munchus House (at 1130 East Terrell Avenue) is a Craftsman-style house from 1922, a two-story wood frame featuring wide, overhanging eaves, stick brackets and prominent gables. The home was built for Dr. George Murry Munchus by a locally prominent black contractor, George Powell. The son of former slaves from Alabama, Munchus was the founder, manager and physician for Fort Worth's Negro Community Hospital.

The Eddleman-McFarland House (at 1110 Penn Street) is a Victorian-designed home built in 1899 for Sarah C. Ball, who was a widow of Galveston banker George Ball. William H. Eddelman bought the home in 1904 and gave it to his daughter in 1921, she being the wife of cattleman Frank H. McFarland. The home's interior still has most of its original woodwork and fixtures, and the exterior has marble, sandstone, brick and copper.

The Edna Gladney House (at 2110 Hemphill) served as an orphanage for abandoned children in Fort Worth and was named after Mrs. Edna Gladney, who became its director in 1910. She became the superintendent for the home in 1927. She worked hard on behalf of orphaned children, and her influence extended into securing legislation and social reform. The home was renamed in her honor in the 1950s. A hospital unit was added in 1954 and was named for veteran board chairman A.J. Duncan. In 1962, the Gladney House was accredited by the Child Welfare League of America, Inc.

The Fairview (or William J. Bryce House, at 4900 Bryce Street) was the house of William Bryce, a native Scotsman, who moved to Fort Worth in 1883, opening a successful brick contracting business. The home was built in 1893 and was designed by the architectural firm of Sanguinet & Messer. Bryce was also the mayor of Fort Worth from 1927 to 1933, and he lived in the home until he died. It is also noted that this home is one of the few chateauesque dwellings in Texas with Richardsonian arches and gabled dormers.

The Garvey-Veihl House (at 769 Samuels Avenue) belonged to a family who moved to the area in the late 1800s and built a home overlooking the Trinity River adjacent to where the current home is located. The Garvey family bought this lot in 1883 and, a year later, built a small one-story frame home, enlarging it over the years. By the late 1890s, it had become a two-story Queen Anne–style home. The house features asymmetrical massing, porches, dormers and beehive turrets. It is one of the many homes that is representative of those on Samuels Avenue at the turn of the century.

The George B. Monnig House (at 115 West Broadway) was the home of George B. Monnig, a merchant in Fort Worth. He and his wife bought this property in 1905, building a two-story frame house. A fire took the home in 1909, so the family replaced it with a tile-roofed brick structure a year later. The home exhibits corbelled brick, milled wood and cut limestone—a blend of bungalow and arts and crafts styles meshed together.

The Gunhild Weber House (at 1404 South Adams) was built in a subdivision back in 1907 and was the first house built by D.T. Bomar and John W. Broad, with West Coast tendencies in design.

The Henry M. Williams House (4926 Crestline Road) was the home of Henry Williams, originally from Georgia, who founded H.W. Williams Wholesale Drug Company in Fort Worth and was also a well-known banker. The house is a Colonial Revival structure built between 1907 and 1909, with portico Corinthian columns and a wide veranda.

The James-Fujita House (at 2530 College Avenue) was built in 1915 for Kanetaro Fujita, president of a Japanese cotton exporting firm, the Gosho Company. He lived in the home until he returned to Japan at the beginning of World War II. The home features a gambrel roof and front porch columns and balusters.

The Laneri House (at 902 South Jennings Avenue) was the home of an Italian immigrant named John B. Laneri, who moved to Fort Worth in 1883 to become a businessman and civic leader. Laneri founded the O.B. Macaroni Company and started a private boys' school, having this home built in 1904 with a brick structure, classical detailing and detailed interior woodwork.

The Lanius House (at 2420 West Adams) was the home of Clarence Lanius, a native of Bonham, Texas, and a cattleman with ranches in a number of locations throughout the state. He and his wife moved to this house about 1922. It's a bungalow style of architecture, with large overhanging and flared eaves. There is also a wide porch and porte-cochere on the façade.

The Marshall R. Sanguinet House (at 4729 Collinwood) was the home of a well-known architect in Fort Worth, Marshall R. Sanguinet, who built this shingle-style house about 1894 and also had his hand in much of the city's early multistory buildings and in the development of the Arlington Heights subdivision, where this home was located.

The Maxwell-Liston House (at 712 May Street) is a late Queen Anne–style home that was built in 1904 by Charles W. Maxwell. He was a contractor and carpenter and lived in the home with his wife until 1907. Features include the corner turret, the wraparound porch and the wreath and scroll decorative work in the front gables.

The Mitchell-Schoonover House (at 600 South Eighth Avenue) was James E. Mitchell's home, finished in 1907 and designed by the Fort Worth architectural firm of Sanguinet & Staats. Mitchell's friend bought the home in 1920 and gave it to his daughter and her husband, Dr. Frank Schoonover, in 1945.

The Pollock-Capps House (at 1120 Penn Street) was built in 1898 for Dr. Joseph R. Pollock and was sold to William Capps and his wife, who lived there until 1971. There is also a golf course, a tennis court and a three-car garage, with a ballroom above, on the property. The neighborhood in which this house is located was nicknamed Quality Hill.

The Rogers-O'Daniel House (at 2230 Warner Road) was built by William Joseph Rogers after he purchased a 137-acre farm here in 1901. It started out as a three-story Queen Anne–style frame structure but was remodeled in 1925 when the farm was subdivided. O'Daniel was the governor of Texas from 1939 to 1941 and served in the U.S. Senate from 1941 to 1949.

The Sandidge-Walker House (at 2420 College Avenue) was owned by cattleman George Sandidge. The house was built about 1921 and was sold four years later to Webb and Gussie Walker. Dr. Walker was the city health official for seven years. In 1954, he sold the home to St. John's Episcopal Church to serve as its rectory. This home features influences of Prairie School–style architecture in its horizontal lines and wide eaves.

The Thomas G. and Marjorie Shaw House (at 2404 Medford Court) is a Monterrey-style house built in 1927 by Fort Worth contractor Bert B. Adams. It is located in the fashionable Park Hill Addition. Features of the home include its stucco wall finish and tile roof.

The William Reeves House (at 2200 Hemphill) was the home of local businessman and philanthropist William Reeves, who built this home beginning in 1907. The home features such characteristics as the Neoclassical Revival and Queen Anne styles of architecture, with a round pavilion at the entrance and a wraparound porches with Doric columns.

Cemeteries that Played a Part

Cemeteries are some of the most valuable historic resources that a city or town can offer its residents and guests. Going back to a time when earlier settlers were forging the future, cemeteries also offer historians a look at settlement patterns with an eye toward how the city has changed over the years. Cemeteries can also tell the story of historic events, religion, lifestyles and genealogy, and Fort Worth's cemeteries are no different. With cemeteries tracing graves back to the families in the area or large groups of settlers buried throughout the years, the city's Pioneers Cemetery, which saw its first grave in 1850, is just one of the many cemeteries in the city that folks can visit to get a bird's-eye view of the history of Fort Worth.

Chapel Cemetery on Old Denton Highway is twenty miles north of Fort Worth, and its origin began with the first settlement in the area in the 1850s, as well as the pioneer family of John A. and Rhoda Raibourn Fanning, Mitchell and Eliny Jane Raibourn and Thomas Raibourn. Fanning family tradition says that the cemetery began with the burial of Eliny Raibourn at this site in 1856, and more land was donated for burial purposes by her brother-in-law, John Fanning. The place was known as the Fanning Burying Grounds for a time, and a one-room schoolhouse known as Horse Creek School or Lone Star School, located a mile south of the cemetery, was the only communal structure in the area until a chapel was built next to the burying grounds. In 1893, the land and chapel were given to the Sweet Chapel Methodist Church, and the burying grounds became known as Sweet Chapel Cemetery. By 1938, the cemetery was being called Chapel Cemetery.

The Ahavath Sholom Hebrew Cemetery on North University was established when the first Jewish Congregation in Fort Worth, Ahavath Sholom, bought six acres of land from the Greenwood Cemetery Association and dedicated the land in 1909. A Ladies Cemetery Society kept the cemetery in order, and the first person was buried here in 1910. In 1929, the cemetery was enlarged, and three soldiers who died in World War II were buried side by side in the northern section of the cemetery. There is also a monument memorializing the millions of Jewish victims of the German Nazi regime in Europe during World War II, erected by members of the congregation who had lost relatives in the Holocaust. The Kornbleet Chapel, with seating for one hundred, was dedicated in 1988.

Ayres Cemetery on Block Scott Street dates back to 1861, when Benjamin Patton Ayres and his wife bought a 320-acre farm, putting aside 2 acres on the hill as a family cemetery. Ayres served as the second Tarrant County clerk and was instrumental in helping to create the Fort Worth First Christian Church. He was the first person buried in Ayres Cemetery. There is also a number of unknown number of graves outside the fenced family plot, include victims of spring fevers and Trinity River floods, the entire cemetery being a reminder of the area's early settlers.

The oldest marked grave in the Birdville pioneer community cemetery is that of Wiley Wilda Potts, who lived from December 1822 to December 1852. The 1.00-acre piece of land was legally set aside for burial purposes before 1860, and later more land was also donated for the same purpose. By 1910, the cemetery was 3.27 acres, and in 1965 the cemetery had 552 known graves. There were a number of families with at least four generations buried in the same plot here. Now the cemetery sits on 7.00 acres and is still actively used for burials.

Burke Cemetery on Bryant Irvine Road saw its first burial in 1867: Mary (Overton) Burke, who came to the area in 1851 with her children and widowed mother to settle the land that had been chosen by her husband. Her mother died two days after she did and was also buried here. In 1900, the one-half acre of land was named as an official family burial ground. There are more than one hundred marked and some unmarked graves at this cemetery.

Fort Worth civic leader John Peter Smith donated land at this site in 1879 for use as a cemetery, called Emanuel Hebrew Rest Cemetery on South Main Street. It was designated for early Jewish residents of the city, and the earliest marked grave is that of a child who died in 1879.

Forest Hill Cemetery on 5713 Forest Hill is one of the oldest burial grounds in Tarrant County and was actually used in the area even before recordkeeping began. It was in 1883 that the property was deeded to the Forest Hill Cumberland Presbyterian Church, and many of the first pioneers are buried here, including Press and Jane Farmer, who lived in the area now called Fort Worth even before the U.S. Army established the fort in 1849. The cemetery has many graves, but most are unmarked or were marked with stones that have since disappeared.

In 1853, Garrett and James Gibson and other family members moved to Tarrant County and established 160-acre homesteads in a settlement that came to be known as the Gibson Community. The Gibson Cemetery on Gibson Cemetery Court was land donated at this site by the family to be used as a cemetery. The earliest marked grave is Garrett Gibson's infant grandson, from 1866. There are about seventy-three marked graves in the cemetery today, and all but a few are relatives of the Gibson family, marked with fieldstones. The cemetery is another reminder of the settlers in the area who were a part of establishing Tarrant County's earliest settlements.

Harrison Cemetery on Meadowbrook Road was at first use a one-acre cemetery belonging to the pioneer D.C. Harrison. The earliest grave is that of Mary E. Harrison, who lived from 1864 to 1871, and other early settlers also used this site for burials. R.A. Randol, the operator of Randol Mill, bought the land in 1895 and deeded it forever as a burial ground. There are now about sixty graves in the cemetery.

The Hitch Cemetery on Kings Port Road is another visible reminder of the early settlers in the area. It was once part of a large farm owned by Kentucky native William Henry Hitch, who came with his family to the area in 1855 from Tennessee. The oldest grave in the cemetery is from 1858, and other than the Hitch family members, the graveyard also contains the burials of relatives in the Trigg, Liggett and Martin families, all of whom had moved to Texas and knew Hitch.

Isham Cemetery at the 7100 block of John T. White Boulevard was donated as a burial ground by Reverend W. Marion Isham and his family, who moved to the area from Georgia in the 1870s. He donated a one-acre plot, and the oldest remaining legible grave marker is from 1870; however, it is documented that earlier burials did take place here, marked with plain sandstone markers. About five acres were added to the graveyard in 1941, and it is still in operation as a community burial ground today.

Oakwood Cemetery on Grand and Gould Avenues was founded in 1879 by John Peter Smith, one of Fort Worth's first settlers and also a civic leader, mayor and philanthropist. Smith donated twenty acres to the city, and since that time the cemetery has been enlarged to one hundred acres, now with three cemeteries: Oakwood, Calvary and Trinity. There are many folks from the Fort Worth and Tarrant County areas, both men and women who were very well known, who are buried in Oakwood Cemetery. Plots are owned by lodges, unions, Catholics, Protestants, blacks and whites, as well as some tracts that are dedicated to Union and Confederate soldiers—even a few prostitutes contribute to the colorful Fort Worth history.

One of those influential citizens worth mentioning was Winfield Scott, who has a mausoleum in the cemetery. Scott, a cattle and oil baron, was buried at Oakwood along with his family. Scott borrowed $500 to purchase his first cattle and then parlayed that into more cattle and then land and oil. Scott and his wife, Elizabeth, were the second owners of Thistle Hill. After purchasing it for $90,000, a huge sum at that time, the Scotts then spent more than $100,000 remodeling. Unfortunately, Scott died before the remodeling was completed, but Elizabeth lived there for twenty-seven years until she passed away in 1938. The chapel was built in 1914.

Almost all of this pioneer cemetery, called Mitchell Cemetery, at Northeast Twenty-eighth and Decatur Avenue, has been erased. There are still about twelve burials that have been identified through written records. First used in the summer of 1848 for the burial of a young child, the cemetery was named for a later owner of the property, Eli Mitchell. There were other Tarrant County pioneers also buried at this cemetery, including John York, who became a county sheriff, and Seaborne Gilmore, a Mexican-American War veteran who was Tarrant County's first elected county judge.

Mount Olivet Cemetery on North Sylvania is about 130 acres in size and was founded in 1907 by Flavious G. McPeak and his wife, who moved to Fort Worth in 1894 from Tennessee. The land where the cemetery is now located was purchased in 1895, and the family built a home there in 1896. When the McPeaks founded the cemetery, they moved to a home on Lake Street. The design of the cemetery is much like the Mount Olivet Cemetery in Nashville, Tennessee, a place that McPeak found had a design he also wanted to incorporate in the one he started in Texas. A mausoleum was completed in 1909 and was torn down when a new mausoleum was built in 1983. There are many freestanding and relief sculptures on the grounds, and the cemetery has more than forty-seven thousand burials. It was the first perpetual care cemetery in the county. The oldest marked grave is from 1907, and the place also interred 594 victims of the flu epidemic of 1918, as well as the McPeaks and many other Tarrant County pioneers.

The Peterson Family Cemetery off IH-35 and Old Denton Road was named after Swedish native John Peterson, who came to the United States in 1868. He and his wife lived in Nebraska before coming to Texas in 1872, and he bought several hundred acres in the area and made a living as a farmer. His granddaughter was the first to be buried in this cemetery in 1903, which now contains ten graves. The site stands as a reminder of Tarrant County's early Swedish settlements.

This burial ground was started in the summer of 1850 upon the deaths of Sophie and Willis Arnold, children of Major Ripley A. Arnold, the commander of the troops at Fort Worth. Pioneers Rest Cemetery at the 600 block Samuels Avenue originally began as a three-acre burial site, but in 1871, after a cemetery association was established, three adjoining acres were added. Many early Fort Worth settlers, including seventy-five Civil War veterans, are buried here; the graves of Major Arnold and General Edward H. Tarrant, whom Tarrant County was named after, are also here.

Willburn Cemetery on Streamwood Road has many of the descendants of Edward Willburn and his wife, Nancy, buried here; they were immigrants who settled in the area in the 1850s. Another pioneer cemetery, the earliest marked grave is from 1867, an infant child. Also buried here are Rachael M. (Wilburn) Snyder, donor of property for a church, school and cemetery in Benbrook; Church Willburn, a cowboy on several cattle drives in the 1860s; Civil War veterans; and other pioneers of southwestern Tarrant County.

Witten Cemetery on Colleyville Circle at Jackson Court was established for the family of Samuel Cecil Holiday Witten, who arrived in Texas in 1854. He was a successful landowner and also served as a justice of the peace and deputy county surveyor. The first use of this cemetery was in 1857, and while Samuel Witten and his wife moved to Corpus Christi in 1890, the cemetery was later used for family descendants.

Chapter 7

NO END IN SIGHT

While no history of Fort Worth would be complete without, well, the history, the amazing thing about this glittering "Cowtown" is that you can still be a part of this story as it replays itself over and over again, especially in the Stockyards area. With the old buildings and remnants (older still) up and down the streets, it's not hard to become lost in a time that existed when Hell's Half Acre and the sound of cattle rustling was just a moment away at any time.

Visitors to Fort Worth these days will notice a lot of changes from years past, but so much of the history is still intact, too. Now known as the "City of Cowboys and Culture," in the downtown area the Heritage Trail offers a series of twenty-two bronze sidewalk markers, concentrated on Main Street from Heritage Park to the Fort Worth Water Gardens. This trail is the first place to stop to take a look at how the city has evolved over the years, both historically and with an eye toward the future, as the trail details Fort Worth's history, people, places and events.

If it's a cattle baron's home you want to visit, then Thistle Hill and the Ball-Eddelman-McFarland House are historical looks at some of the city's finest. Thistle Hill was built in 1903 and is a very well-restored Georgian Revival mansion. The Ball-Eddelman-McFarland House was built in 1899 and is a Queen Anne–style home.

In Fort Worth's Sundance Square/downtown area, much has changed over the years. With Broadway-style shows at the seraph-fronted Bass Performance Hall, plays at the African American Jubilee Theatre or intimate performances at the cabaret-sized McDavid Studio, Fort Worth

The Wild West mingles with modernity. *Photo by Russell William Dandridge.*

A Stockyards street scene, where saloons still rule the day, 2011. *Photo by Russell William Dandridge.*

has definitely become the cultural institution it always dreamed of being back in the early days. With the five distinct world-class museums anchored in a park-like setting in Fort Worth's cultural district—the Amon Carter Museum, the Fort Worth Museum of Science and History, the Kimbell Art Museum, the Modern Art Museum of Fort Worth and the National Cowgirl Museum and Hall of Fame—there is something for everyone, no matter the taste. The Texas Motor Speedway, home to both NASCAR and IndyCar racing events each year, is also nearby and is a huge draw. There is also more shopping than those folks in the 1800s Fort Worth could have ever imagined.

Of course, some of the best shopping is found in the Stockyards at Stockyards Station. This area of Fort Worth is where the city really began, and today you can still enjoy the rich history while shopping and dining in the area. Located in the heart of the Fort Worth Stockyards, Stockyards Station offers a good blend of past and present, and you can also opt for a historic walking tour from the station as well. With twenty-five shops, including a winery, an art gallery and restaurants, here are a few ideas of where to begin.

Another big coup for the city was the chance to re-create Trinity River and its surroundings. In many places, the old houses and the less-than-good parts of town have given way to new developments, and the Trinity River area is now a vibrant waterfront offering the hopes of condominiums, restaurants, shops and entertainment, just one more piece of the Fort Worth puzzle. Even now, it's interesting to note that at the Pier 1 Place, a large glass building sits nearby

A cowboy Cadillac in front of the Stockyard's water tower, 2011. *Photo by Russell William Dandridge.*

81

Stockyards Station. *Photo by Russell William Dandridge.*

where it all began, and the thirty-eight-acre Radio Shack campus also sits on the bluff where that first military post was established in the late 1840s. It's a future that one could only have imagined.

Even more exciting, as in years past when the oil boom hit, about 27 trillion cubic feet of natural gas has been found recently in Tarrant County, as well as other counties nearby—another boon perhaps.

Where to go now? As in the 1800s and 1900s, Fort Worth is a city with a history that it embraces and a future that grows only stronger, with its ability to enjoy and take pride in things and learn from its past.

United States Mint

Another significant impact that Fort Worth has had on not only surrounding cities but also the United States is the United States Mint located in Fort Worth. Visitors can still take free tours of this working facility. With billions of dollars at the Bureau of Engraving and Printing (aka the Mint) located in Fort Worth, it is a part of the U.S. Department of the Treasury.

The tour and visitor center is a state-of-the-art facility and is a part of one of only two locations in the world where United States paper currency is printed. Guided tours are offered at the Fort Worth Western Currency Facility location on a regular basis; indeed it is a place where the phrase "show me the money" is real. Responsible for the design, engraving and printing of all U.S. paper currency, the Bureau of Engraving and Printing (BEP) in Fort Worth produces more than half of the nation's currency. On production days, a whopping $26 million in currency is produced per hour here, and the paper currency is still made of 75 percent cotton and 25 percent linen.

Even though it's made to be tough—reportedly requiring up to four thousand double folds, first forward and then backward, before a note will tear—the U.S. currency still has a pretty short life span, with a one-dollar bill lasting about twelve months and a five-dollar bill only about sixteen months.

Visitors to BEP first take a forty-five-minute tour beginning on the first of two floors, with a number of interesting interactive exhibits and displays that are dedicated to the history of U.S. paper currency, as well as the history of the BEP, both in Fort Worth and Washington D.C.

Also featured on the first level is a recently restored and fully operational turn-of-the-century spider press, as well as more recent additions, including the chance to touch various engraved plates and the opportunity to attempt to figure out the million-dollar "Do the Math" display. Still need more? There's the graduated "tower" of shredded currency called "How Tall Are You Worth?" Before heading to the next level, maybe you'll want to purchase a bit of your own uncut currency at the Moneyfactory Gift Shop.

A short elevator ride later, the second level is home to a seventy-five-seat theater, where a fourteen-minute, hi-definition educational film on the production of currency called *The Buck Starts Here* allows visitors a chance to understand how it's all done. After the film, it's time for the highlight: a guided tour on the quarter-mile-long enclosed and elevated walkway overlooking the currency production floor.

If you still haven't had enough, after the guided portion of the tour there are still more chances for interaction, including an exhibit on plate making and engraving, offset, intaglio plate printing and mechanical examination, as well as ending with a look at BEP's packaging operations. Continuously looped worker videos also showcase interviews with various production employees and allow for a chance to actually see the sights and hear the sounds on the production floor.

A giant twenty-dollar bill turns sequentially in the order of the production process, beginning with the paper layer. Various text and photo panels give details about the paper and ink used in making U.S. currency. A mutilated currency redemption area on the second level provides information as to what is involved in the redemption of mutilated money.

The Bureau of Engraving and Printing is located on 9000 Blue Mound Road in Fort Worth, Texas. You can call 817-231-4000 or toll-free at 866-865-1194 for more information.

The secretary of the U.S. Treasury is responsible for the selection of the designs, including the portraits, that appear on paper currency. The portraits currently appearing on the various denominations of paper currency were adopted in 1929, when the size of the notes was reduced. Can you name who is featured in the portraits on our current U.S. paper currency?

- $1 note—face: George Washington (first U.S. president); back: the Great Seal of the United States.
- $2 note—face: Thomas Jefferson (third U.S. president); back: signing of the Declaration of Independence.
- $5 note—face: Abraham Lincoln (sixteenth U.S. president); back: Lincoln Memorial.
- $10 note—face: Alexander Hamilton (first secretary of the treasury); back: U.S. Treasury Building.
- $20 note—face: Andrew Jackson (seventh U.S. president); back: White House.
- $50 note—face: Ulysses Grant (eighteenth U.S. president); back: U.S. Capitol.
- $100 note—face: Ben Franklin (statesman); back: Independence Hall.

What about the names of those featured on the higher-dollar currency notes, which are no longer in print or circulation?

- $500 note—face: William McKinley (twenty-fifth U.S. president); back: the numeral "500" and the ornamental phrase "Five Hundred Dollars."
- $1,000 note—face: Grover Cleveland (twenty-second and twenty-fourth U.S. president); back: the numeral "1,000" and the ornamental phrase "One Thousand Dollars."
- $5,000 note—face: James Madison (fourth U.S. president); back: the numeral "5,000" and the ornamental phrase "Five Thousand Dollars."
- $10,000 note—face: Salmon Chase (U.S. Treasury secretary under Lincoln); back: the numeral "10,000" and the ornamental phrase "Ten Thousand Dollars."
- $100,000 note—face: Woodrow Wilson (twenty-eighth U.S. president); back: the numeral "100,000" and the ornamental phrase "One Hundred Thousand Dollars." This note never appeared in general circulation and was only used in transactions between Federal Reserve Banks.

THINGS TO DO AND PLACES TO SEE

With so much to see and do in Fort Worth, depending on your favorite activities, the Stockyards area is certainly worth a few days, but don't miss the art galleries and museums that are a part of the city, too. With so much good food—think Tex-Mex and barbecue—you can bet you won't go hungry. There's a dose of culture, a bit of shopping and a good beer (yes, you can still walk around with alcohol in the Stockyards area as you go from bar to bar), but other than that, just close your eyes, breathe in the history and have a good time.

In the Stockyards

Billy Bob's Texas
2520 Rodeo Plaza
Fort Worth, Texas
817-624-7117

Celebrating its thirtieth anniversary on April 1, 2011, Billy Bob's Texas is the world's largest honky-tonk, set on three acres. With an indoor rodeo arena for professional bull riding, a Texas-size dance floor, dozens of bar stations, restaurants, arcade games, a Wall of Fame with celebrity handprints and a general store.

One of many old signs, this one designates a boot maker, 2011. *Photo by Russell William Dandridge.*

The Bluebonnet Room
2507 Rodeo Plaza
Fort Worth, Texas
817-822-9116

The Bluebonnet Room, located in the historic La Plaza Building, was constructed in 1911 and features a dance floor and access to a private balcony overlooking a creek.

Booger Red's Saloon
105 East Exchange Avenue

Fort Worth, Texas
817-624-1246

If you are visiting H3 Ranch, stop at Booger Red's Saloon, named in honor of the legendary Texas bronc-busting champion Samuel Thomas Privett (1858–1926). A Stockyards district institution since 1984, Booger Red's features Fort Worth's most complete selection of tequilas, the one-of-a-kind "Anita-Rita" margarita and the sixteen-ounce Buffalo Butt Beer, named for the aft end of the mighty beast prominently mounted in the center of Booger Red's bar.

The Bull Ring

112 East Exchange Avenue
Fort Worth, Texas
817-624-2222

The Bull Ring serves handmade ice cream and a wide variety of beer by the bottle. But what makes this establishment one of the most unique places in Fort Worth is its impressive collection of great early Texas art (1845–1965). It is said that there is not a better collection of such art in all of Fort Worth.

The Cantina Cadillac

124 West Exchange Avenue
Fort Worth, Texas
817-625-6622

Fort Worth, Texas's premier rodeo hot spot, where real cowboy's come to life from Thursday through Sunday.

Cowtown Cattlepen Maze

145 East Exchange Avenue
Fort Worth, Texas
817-624-6666

The Cowtown Cattlepen Maze is a unique form of entertainment with more than 5,400 square feet of frequently changed wooden pathways, resembling the cattle pens of the Old West. The maze is always a challenge. Maze runners can compete against the clock and against one another, attempting to locate checkpoints throughout the maze in a given time, to qualify for Amaze'n Prizes. The large, second-story observation deck provides the opportunity to preview the maze before entering.

Cowtown Coliseum
121 East Exchange Avenue
Fort Worth, Texas
888-269-8696 (C-O-W-T-O-W-N)
817-624-4711

In 1986, the Cowtown Coliseum was totally refurbished and brought up to modern-day standards, including heating and air conditioning systems, as well as production lighting and sound. It is the home to rodeo events every Friday and Saturday night year-round.

The Cowtown Opry
131 East Exchange Avenue, #140
Fort Worth, Texas
817-366-9675

A nonprofit organization dedicated to the preservation of country music as a part of Texas heritage, the Cowtown Opry provides for one of the most authentic western experiences in the area. With free weekly concerts held outside on the steps of the Livestock Exchange Building, it's almost like taking a time machine back into the days of cattle driving and saloons.

Filthy McNasty's Saloon
114 West Exchange Avenue
Fort Worth, Texas
817-386-0170

Filthy McNasty's is one block west of Main Street and has been a part of Fort Worth's western heritage and local music scene for three generations.

Jersey Lilly Old Time Photo Parlor
128 East Exchange Avenue, Barn A
Fort Worth Texas
817-626-7131

Located in the Texas Cowboy Hall of Fame in the Fort Worth Stockyards, you can get antique sepia-tone photos of the Old West with four different backgrounds, including a real stagecoach, as well as costumes and props.

La Plaza Building
2501–2519 Rodeo Plaza
Fort Worth, Texas
817-744-7881

The La Plaza Building was constructed in 1911 and was called the Exhibit Building; it was an exhibit hall for farm implements. Later the building was used by Frank Kent Cadillac and, during World War II, by Lockheed Martin. The great flood of Fort Worth washed away half of the building, leaving it the size it is today. During the Vietnam War era, the building was used by Bell Helicopter and was finally restored as a retail establishment in the mid-1980s.

Livestock Exchange Building
131 East Exchange Avenue
Fort Worth, Texas

Located in the Fort Worth Stockyards, this adobe-style building was constructed in 1902 as a center for cattle traders. It was the central location for all activity in the Stockyards and is often referred to as "the Wall Street of the West." Today, the building houses professional services and the North Fort Worth Historical Society Museum, which features artifacts from the beginning of the development of the Stockyards.

Pawnee Bill's Wild West Show
121 East Exchange
Fort Worth, Texas

This is a historical reenactment of the original Pawnee Bill's Wild West Show, with trick roping, trick shooting, trick riding, cowboy songs and an entertaining look at history. Historical figures such as Pawnee Bill come to life and transport the spectator back in time, and the shows are based on actual events and stunts that occurred in the original Pawnee Bill's Wild West Show that toured the country some ninety years ago.

Pearl's Dancehall & Saloon

302 West Exchange Avenue
Fort Worth, Texas
817-624-2800

When Buffalo Bill Cody showed up at the Fort Worth Stockyards in the late 1800s, he decided that the area's night life was lacking, so he went ahead and built a bordello and named it Hotel Pearl's. The entry parlor of what is now Pearl's Dancehall & Saloon still has pieces of Buffalo Bill's vision scattered about, including the original pressed-tin gold ceilings that have been restored and historically marked, plus a nude portrait of the grand madam herself that adorns the blood-red wall to your left as you walk in. Nowadays, you can enjoy traditional country, honky-tonk and western swing music and a long, copper-sheet metal bar with an ornate mahogany back.

Rodeo Exchange Club

221 West Exchange Avenue
Fort Worth, Texas
817-626-0181

The Rodeo Exchange Club is in the Stockyards at the top of the hill at West Exchange and North Houston and has live bands on Friday and Saturday.

Stockyards Championship Rodeo

121 East Exchange Avenue
Fort Worth, Texas
817-625-1025

There's a rodeo every Friday and Saturday night at 8:00 p.m., with bull riding, bareback riding, tie-down roping, team roping and barrel racing.

Stockyards Museum
131 East Exchange Avenue (Stockyards)
Fort Worth, Texas 76164
817-625-5082

This is a historic site offering visitors an opportunity to explore the history of Fort Worth and how it was developed from a stop for cowboys driving cattle north to the stock market of the West that sold millions of heads of cattle and then shipped them by railroad. It is home to the second-oldest antique light bulb, still illuminated. The Stockyards Museum is located in the classic 1903 Livestock Exchange Building in the heart of the Fort Worth Stockyards National Historic District. The North Fort Worth Historical Society first opened the Stockyards Museum in 1989.

Stockyards National Historic District
140 East Exchange Avenue
Fort Worth, Texas

The Texas Trail of Fame was established to honor those who have made a significant contribution to our western way of life. Throughout the walkways of the Fort Worth Stockyards National Historic District, bronze inlaid markers have been placed around in honor of their achievements and to inspire and educate visitors by reflecting on these western accomplishments.

Stockyards Station Gallery
140 East Exchange Avenue (Stockyards), #113
Fort Worth, Texas 76164
817-624-7300

The Stockyards Gallery has a large collection of fine art, including original bronzes, paintings, creative home furnishings, rope art, iron carvings and more.

Stockyards Visitor Information Center
130 East Exchange Avenue
Fort Worth, Texas
817-624-4711

A great way to experience Fort Worth's history, the Stockyards was once the second-largest cattle market in the world. Nowadays you will find a number of entertainment options, with restaurants, shopping and Wild West performances. Annual events include the Red Steagall Cowboy Gathering and Frontier Forts Days. Daily cattle drive times are 11:30 a.m. and 4:00 p.m. Drives are not held on Easter Sunday, Thanksgiving Day or Christmas Day.

Stockyards Walking Tour
130 East Exchange Avenue
Fort Worth, Texas
817-625-9715

Take a historical walking tour and learn about the colorful history of the Fort Worth Stockyards. Walking tours visit these historic locations in the Stockyards: the Historic Livestock Exchange Building, Stockyards Station, the cattlemen's catwalk, Mule Alley, Billy Bob's Texas and the Texas Trail of Fame.

Texas Cowboy Hall of Fame
128 East Exchange Avenue (Stockyards), #100
Fort Worth, Texas 76164
817-626-7131

The Texas Cowboy Hall of Fame is a tribute to the top cowboys and cowgirls who have excelled in the sports of rodeo, cutting and ranching, as well as those individuals who have dedicated their lives to promoting and preserving Texas western heritage. When visiting the Hall of Fame, visitors have a chance to experience the Old West by exploring the Sterquell Wagon collection with more than sixty wagons, carts, buddies and sleighs. And little ones will love the Exploratorium, where they can learn to pack for a trail drive and dig for treasures in the sawdust, among other hands-on experiences. The Texas Cowboy Hall of Fame was opened in 2001, is one of the horse and mule barns of the Stockyards historic district that was originally built in 1888 and at one time housed more than three thousand horses and mules.

Texas Rodeo Cowboy Hall of Fame
121 East Exchange Avenue
Fort Worth, Texas 76164

Located in the historic Fort Worth Stockyards at Cowtown Coliseum, this organization is dedicated to the sport of rodeo and the recognition of Texas's contribution to that sport. It was founded in 1975 by Johnny Boren and a group of Belton, Texas businessmen. Boren was the manager of the Professional Rodeo Cowboys Association (PRCA) Lone Star Circuit, the biggest circuit in the PRCA's circuit system. Every year in April, champion cowboys who made an impact on the sport in Texas are honored at the very popular reunion ceremony.

White Elephant Saloon
106 East Exchange Avenue
Fort Worth, Texas 76102
817-624-9712

Billed as "a place to see how the real West was, and still is," the White Elephant Saloon is a little slice of history in a thoroughly modern world. The saloon hosts a variety of electric and acoustical country acts, as well as a scenic outdoor beer garden stage that is hopping in the spring months. The White Elephant is one of the marquee establishments in the Stockyards.

HISTORICAL PLACES TO VISIT

Fire Station No. 1
203 Commerce Street (downtown)
Fort Worth, Texas 76102
817-732-1631

Free of charge to visit, Fire Station No. 1 is a historic fire station near Fort Worth's Sundance Square. There is an excellent exhibit in the station that commemorates the first 150 years of Fort Worth, from its beginning as a frontier outpost and through its rowdy youth as a cattle town to the present day. Built in 1907, features include an interactive bunkhouse model featuring a video about Charlie Bell, a well-known Texas cowboy who spent a lifetime working cattle; a scale model of the original Fort Worth, established in 1849; a display case containing the uniform and writing desk of Major General William Jenkins Worth, Fort Worth's namesake; a display on the prehistoric Clovis people; and a bucking bronco that provides a photo opportunity for guests. Fire Station No. 1 is also a part of the Fort Worth Museum of Science and History.

Log Cabin Village
2100 Log Cabin Village Lane (cultural district)
Fort Worth, Texas 76109
817-392-5881

With historical interpreters at the helm, guests can experience the sights, sounds and smells of nineteenth-century Texas on three acres in Fort Worth. Log Cabin Village consists of nine historic structures dating back to the mid-1800s. You can experience Texas history through authentic log homes and artifacts, a blacksmith shop, a one-room schoolhouse, a smokehouse, a water-powered gristmill and an herb garden. The historical interpreters will also demonstrate various frontier chores, like candle making, spinning and weaving. The Log Cabin Village also collects, preserves and exhibits an eclectic collection of objects, documents and structures related to north Texas history from 1840 through 1890. The objects include textiles, tools, equipment, furniture and personal artifacts. Six log houses, dating back to the mid-1800s, were selected from the north Texas region, moved to the present site and restored in the 1950s to early 1960s. Each of the historic structures, furnished with authentic artifacts, displays different aspects of pioneer life.

Thistle Hill
1110 Penn Street
Fort Worth, Texas
817-332-5875

Near the city's hospital district, this Georgian Revival–style mansion has been restored to its 1912 condition and is listed on the National Register of Historic Places. The nearly eleven-thousand-square-foot, red brick structure was once the scene of lavish dinners and parties when the Whartons entertained Fort Worth's powerful and elite.

RESTAURANTS

Cattlemen's Fort Worth Steak House
2458 North Main Street
Fort Worth, Texas
817-624-3945

Since 1947, Cattlemen's internationally famous steakhouse serves various cuts of meat in an authentic western environment. You can also watch your steak being cooked on the charcoal broiler, and there is an extensive beer and wine list.

Cattlemen's Fort Worth Steak House, 2011. *Photo by Russell William Dandridge.*

H3 Ranch

105 East Exchange Avenue
Fort Worth, Texas
817-624-1246

Breakfast, lunch or dinner at H3 Ranch is cooked on a hickory wood grill. Each day, spit-roasted pig and chicken turn on the open rotisserie, and trout, ribs and steaks are also served, as well as the famous H3 appetizer dip "Nine Miles of Dirt Road." Desserts are homemade pies, and cobblers are baked fresh daily.

Habanero's Mexican Restaurant

817-566-0917

Habanero's specializes in fresh, authentic Mexican food and tasty margaritas. Some of the favorite menu items include fajitas (beef or chicken), camarones calientes (spicy shrimp), bacon-wrapped shrimp stuffed with Monterey Jack cheese and carne asada, a grilled, hand-cut rib eye steak with rich spices.

Lonesome Dove Western Bistro

2406 North Main Street
Fort Worth, Texas
817-740-8810

Opened in 2000, the Lonesome Dove Western Bistro offers urban western dining with celebrity chef Tim Love at the helm.

Los Vaqueros Restaurant

2629 North Main Street
Fort Worth, Texas
817-625-1511

Owned by the Cisneros family, this was once a 1915 packinghouse, personally restored to house this restaurant. Using fresh food daily, fajitas are hand-trimmed, tenderized and marinated without the use of enzymes. Fresh chicken stock is prepared daily in the kitchen and used in various Los Vaqueros recipes. Fresh produce, never frozen, bagged or prechopped, is used as well.

Love Shack
110 East Exchange Avenue
Fort Worth, Texas
817-740-8812

A place where you can get "the best burger in Fort Worth," or so it's noted. Chef Tim Love's outdoor burger joint always draws a crowd.

Riscky's BBQ Steakhouse
817-626-7777

Riscky's BBQ has been around for more than seventy-five years, serving up the finest in mouthwatering ribs, barbecue sandwiches and chicken. The world-renowned Riscky's barbecue is hand-rubbed with "Riscky Dust" and slow-smoked for hours. According to the folks who work at Riscky's and the customers who frequent the restaurants, Riscky's has become a legend in Texas barbecue.

Riscky's BBQ Steakhouse, 2011. *Photo by Russell William Dandridge.*

The Star Café
111 West Exchange
Fort Worth, Texas
817-624-8701

The Star Café was built in the early 1900s and wears its original charm like a Texas badge of honor. From the tin ceiling to the countertops, the Star Café offers a nostalgic trip back to days long ago; it is family owned and operated.

Trailboss Burgers
817-625-1070

Trailboss Burgers is an addition to the Riscky's family of restaurants and serves burgers in the Stockyards, including buffalo burgers.

TOURS

Cowtown Segway Tours
1501 Montgomery Street
Fort Worth, Texas
817-255-9540

From Fort Worth's establishment in 1849 to Fort Worth's present, pioneering spirit and determination can still be seen, and Cowtown Segway Tours will give you a glimpse into the past by guiding and gliding among Fort Worth's cultural district, downtown Sundance Square, Trinity Uptown or the "Old Town" Stockyards. Knowledgeable guides offers interesting stories and facts centered on the astonishing architecture and historical landmarks.

Customized Bus Tours
4048 Ridglea Country Club Drive, #1208
Fort Worth, Texas
817-731-3875

This is a guided walking tour of Fort Worth from its founding to its present-day revitalization. Customized bus tours include sites visited such as historic homes, buildings and more. Have an expert on Fort Worth's rich history join your group for lunch or dinner and weave tales of Fort Worth then and now.

Heritage Trail
Downtown Fort Worth, Texas

You can have your photo taken with a sleeping panther and visit each permanent bronze plaque detailing a historic event that occurred.

Walking History Tour
PO Box 821923
Fort Worth, Texas
817-514-9567

Walk the history of Fort Worth and get up close and personal with the history of the city on a two-hour driving/walking tour that takes you back in time to help you see why Fort Worth has been called the "Queen City of the Prairie." Tours are two hours and feature a mix of walking and driving. Along the way, you will have a chance to see sites and historical markers, including:

1) the bluff near original Fort Worth
2) the historical marker of Fort Worth's first school
3) Tarrant County Courthouse
4) the original site of City Marshal "Long-haired" Jim Courtright's city jail
5) Hell's Half Acre
6) John Swartz's photography studio
7) the site of the old Westbrook Hotel
8) Daggett's Crossing
9) Pioneer Rest Cemetery
10) Billy Bob's Texas honky-tonk
11) the historic Stockyards district (all buildings, markers and stories)
12) North Fort Worth Historical Society Museum
13) Joe T. Garcia's restaurant
14) Northside High School
15) LaGrave Field
16) Paddock Viaduct

17) Fort Worth Power & Light Company Plant

18) Burk Burnet Building

19) Blackstone Hotel

20) W.T. Waggoner Building

21) the *Fort Worth Star Telegram* building

22) Flatiron Building

23) Ball-Eddleman-McFarland House

24) Thistle Hill

25) F.G. Oxsheer mansion

26) Texas Hotel (Hilton)

27) Panther Park

In addition to many historical places, this tour will also give you some interesting information on some of the most interesting Fort Worth–related folks, including John Peter Smith; Buckley Paddock; Major Arnold Ripley; General William Jenkins Worth; General Edward H. Tarrant; E.M. Daggett; B.C. Evans; Luke Short; "Long-haired" Jim Courtright; the members of the Wild Bunch; Butch Cassidy and the Sundance Kid; Etta Place (was she a schoolteacher, a cousin or a soiled dove?); John Swartz; Wyatt Earp; Doc Holliday; Bat Masterson; Fannie Porter; Quanah Parker; Cynthia Parker; Waddy Ross (Ross Brothers Horse & Mule Dealers); Charles McFarland; Bill Pickett; President Theodore Roosevelt; Major K.M. van Zandt; M.B. Loyd; F.G. Oxsheer; William "Gooseneck" McDonald; General Thomas N. Waul, CSA; W.T. Waggoner; Electra Waggoner; Samuel Burk Burnett; Winfield and Elizabeth Scott; the McLaury brothers; General Carswell; J. Frank Norris; and Amon G. Carter Sr.

Museums and Art Galleries

Adobe Western Art Gallery
2322 North Main Street (Stockyards/Northside)
Fort Worth, Texas
817-624-4242

Adobe Western Art Gallery offers both traditional and contemporary fine western art, western sculpture, jewelry and pottery, including a fine selection of western furniture.

American Airlines C.R. Smith Museum
4601 Highway 360 (east side of the city)
Fort Worth, Texas
817-967-1560

The American Airlines C.R. Smith Museum is one of the few museums in the world dedicated solely to commercial aviation. It's a sight-and-sound, hands-on, window-seat look at the world of flight.

Amon Carter Museum of American Art
3501 Camp Bowie Boulevard (cultural district)
Fort Worth, Texas 76107
817-738-1933

This is a free museum with some amazing American art, including the first landscape painters of the 1830s up through modern artists of the twentieth century. The museum was designed by the Glass House creator, Phillip Johnson, who is also known for winning the Pritzker Architecture Prize. You will also find here founder Amon Carter's collection of works by the two greatest artists of the American West: Frederic Remington and Charles M. Russell. Other works include illustrated books, Carter's rare collection of literature published during the past two centuries, nearly four thousand square feet of gallery space devoted to the ongoing display of its photography holdings, an important collection of American sculpture and collections of drawings, prints and watercolors.

Art on the Boulevard
4319-A Camp Bowie Boulevard (cultural district)
Fort Worth, Texas
817-737-6368

Art on the Boulevard is a cooperative gallery, with artwork styles ranging from abstract expressionism to photorealism. There are five major shows per year: Valentine's Show, Spring Gallery Night, Mid-Summer Show, Fall Gallery Night and the Holiday Show.

Carol Henderson Gallery

6387 Camp Bowie Boulevard (cultural district)
Fort Worth, Texas
817-763-8239

Beginning in 1989, the Carol Henderson Gallery has made a commitment to exhibit and market the finest eclectic collection of art to be found. That commitment has remained the focus of this well-known gallery.

Edmund Craig Gallery

3550 West Seventh Street (cultural district)
Fort Worth, Texas
817-732-6663

The Edmund Craig Gallery offers a wide variety of original works from local, national and international artists, including paintings, sculpture and handcrafted jewelry, in a relaxed casual atmosphere. The gallery has, on average, eight shows per year, and the art ranges from representational to abstract.

Evelyn Siegel Gallery

3700 West Seventh Street (downtown)
Fort Worth, Texas
817-731-6412

This gallery features twentieth-century art by local, national and international artists. On display are paintings, prints, ceramics, sculpture, pottery, folk art, glass and Native American artifacts.

Fort Worth Community Arts Center

1309 Montgomery Street (cultural district)
Fort Worth, Texas
817-738-1938

The Fort Worth Community Arts Center's mission is to provide accessible and affordable exhibition, performance, workshop, classroom and office spaces to artists and arts organizations in the region, as well as to serve the general public by presenting the work of contemporary visual and performing artists.

Fort Worth Museum of Science and History
1600 Gendy Street
Fort Worth, Texas
817-255-9300

Adding to the architectural legacy of Fort Worth's cultural district, the Fort Worth Museum of Science and History's brand-new $80 million facility is dazzling, with its bright colors, geometric forms and abundant natural light. Designed by internationally acclaimed architectural firm Legorreta + Legorreta, the new facility was opened in November 2009. To strengthen the museum's presentation of history, the expansion incorporates a major new center for the Cattle Raisers Museum. Exhibits also include DinoLabs; *Paluxysaurus jonesi*, the official dinosaur of Texas; the Noble Planetarum; the Fort Worth Children's Museum; Innovation Studios; six glass-walled spaces near the main entrance offering hands-on demonstrations; and the Omni Imax Theater.

Galerie Kornye West
1601 Clover Lane (cultural district)
Fort Worth, Texas
817-763-5227

Galerie Kornye West offers original fine art, oil paintings, bronzes, ceramics and drawings in impressionistic and academic styles. The Galerie represents well-established living artists engaged in the current arena of American representational art.

Gallery 414
414 Templeton (cultural district)
Fort Worth, Texas
817-336-6595

Gallery 414 was opened in September 1995. Promoting and exhibiting contemporary art in a variety of media and subject matter, it offers an alternative, noncommercial art space showing a mixture of talented artists both known and new to Fort Worth art patrons.

Heliotrope
3461-B Bluebonnet Circle (Hulen/South area)
Fort Worth, Texas
817-924-1113

An American contemporary craft gallery that offers a venue for local artists to introduce and share their work with the public.

Kimbell Art Museum
3333 Camp Bowie Boulevard
Fort Worth, Texas
817-332-8451

The Kimbell's permanent collection contains holdings ranging from the third millennium BC to the mid-twentieth century and includes major works by Fra Angelico, Velazquez, Bernini, Rembrandt, Goya, Monet, Cézanne, Picasso, Mondrian and Matisse. It is also home to Michelangelo's first painting. The collection comprises Asian, non-western and European art. In addition to the permanent collection, the museum features special exhibits on display throughout the year. Designed by world-renowned architect Louis Kahn, the museum is often referred to as one of the most epic structures of the twentieth century.

Leonard's Department Store Museum
200 Carroll Street
Fort Worth, Texas
817-336-9111

It's free admission into this museum, which has photographs of the store and its employees, memorabilia like a popcorn machine and store advertisements and even a piece of the store escalator. Leonard's Department Store is another institution that entertained and charmed Fort Worth shoppers for years—now it is a museum and a piece of history that shaped the city.

Milan Gallery

505 Houston (downtown)
Fort Worth, Texas
817-338-4278

A fine art gallery representing local, national and international artists. More than two hundred pieces of original artwork are displayed.

Modern Art Museum of Fort Worth

3200 Darnell Street
Fort Worth, Texas
817-738-9215

World-renowned architect Tadao Ando's "Arbor for Art," the Modern Art Museum of Fort Worth is a striking building that embodies the pure, unadorned elements of a modern work of art. It is composed of five pavilions of concrete and glass, set on eleven naturally landscaped acres, including a 1.5-acre reflecting pond. The Modern maintains one of the foremost collections of postwar art in the central United States, consisting of more than three thousand significant works of modern and contemporary international art.

Monnig Meteorite Gallery at TCU

Sid W. Richardson Science Building Bowie Street at University Drive (University area)
2950 West Bowie Street
Fort Worth, Texas
817-257-6277

Explore the mysteries of meteorites and experience a hands-on encounter with different types, as well as create your own terrestrial impact crater. You can even see rare meteorites from Mars and a collection found in Texas.

National Cowgirl Museum and Hall of Fame
1720 Gendy (cultural district)
Fort Worth, Texas 76107
817-336-4475

The National Cowgirl Museum and Hall of Fame is the only museum in the world honoring women of the American West who have displayed extraordinary courage and a pioneering spirit in their trailblazing efforts. The museum offers a rare photograph collection, various artifacts, a theater and a Wild West–themed gift shop.

Sid Richardson Museum
309 Main Street (downtown)
Sundance Square
Fort Worth, Texas 76102
817-332-6554

With free admission to the Sid Richardson Museum, visitors can enjoy a large collection of western art, including that of Frederic Remington and Charles M. Russell. Located in downtown's historic Sundance Square, the museum is named after oil mogul Sid Richardson, once known as the "bachelor billionaire," and is considered one of the finest and most focused collections of Western art in America. Sid Richardson began collecting the works of Remington and Russell with the help of Newhouse Galleries of New York City. Newhouse became Richardson's principal dealer and helped him acquire the majority of his paintings.

Texas Civil War Museum
760 North Jim Wright Freeway
Fort Worth, Texas
817-246-2323

The largest Civil War museum west of the Mississippi River features weapons, uniforms, artifacts and Victorian-era dresses from the Civil War. It also houses a theater that shows videos about Texas's involvement in the Civil War.

Thomas Kinkade Gallery
302 Main Street (downtown)
Fort Worth, Texas
817-335-1140

Thomas Kinkade is America's most collected living artist, a painter-communicator whose tranquil, light-infused paintings have delighted millions over the years. This gallery carries Kinkade's work exclusively and offers one of the most extensive collections, including originals and limited edition work.

Vintage Flying Museum
505 Northwest Thirty-eighth Street, Hangar 33 South
Fort Worth, Texas
817-624-1935

Twenty aircraft are on exhibit here, including several that are extremely rare and historic. Additional displays include a dedicated reciprocal and jet engine room, an FAA Aviation Education Resource Center, World War II memorabilia and artifact exhibits, a unique aircraft model exhibit and a gift shop.

William Campbell Contemporary Art
4935 Byers Avenue (cultural district)
Fort Worth, Texas
817-737-9566

Here is collected contemporary paintings, drawings, original prints, photography, sculpture and ceramics by nationally recognized and emerging artists from Texas. Fine art appraisals are also made here by a certified member of American Society of Appraisers.

MISCELLANEOUS

Beaumont Ranch
10736 County Road 102
Grandview, Texas
817-866-4867

Beaumont Ranch is an eight-hundred-acre working cattle ranch specializing in corporate and private client entertainment, with a herd of Texas longhorns, horses, two twenty-thousand-square-foot event barns, a bed-and-breakfast and cowboys. The location is close to Fort Worth and is the perfect meeting spot, which is one of the many reasons Ron and Linda Beaumont purchased the property. There are nine houses with six families living on the ranch, including four generations of Beaumonts. The ranch is also home to an authentic western town, a horse barn and miles of breathtaking scenery.

Fort Worth Water Gardens
1502 Commerce Street
Fort Worth, Texas
817-392-7111

The Fort Worth Water Gardens is an oasis adjacent to the Fort Worth Convention Center. Designed by Phillip Johnson, the Water Gardens is an architectural and engineering marvel to be enjoyed any time of the year.

Rahr & Sons Brewing Company
701 Galveston Avenue
Fort Worth, Texas
817-810-9266

The story of Rahr & Sons Brewing Company really started when Fritz Rahr graduated from Texas Christian University. Fortunately for beer lovers in north Texas, Fritz fell in love not only with Fort Worth but also with his future wife here. And in another fortuitous twist for all of us, Fritz's wife, Erin, gave him the thumbs up when he announced that he would like to carry on the Rahr family tradition of brewing. Fritz and Erin founded Rahr & Sons Brewing Company in the fall of 2004. In five years, the brewery has more than doubled its brewing capacity—from two thousand barrels per year to more than five thousand barrels per year—and has won fifteen nationally recognized awards, including a bronze medal at the 2008 World Beer Cup for Bucking Bock and the 2009 National Grand Champion award from the United States Beer Tasting Championships for Iron Thistle.

Texas Motor Speedway
3545 Lone Star Circle
Fort Worth, Texas
817-215-8593

Three times a year, the auto racing world converges on Texas Motor Speedway, where fans watch the fastest things on four wheels. In April, NASCAR brings its show to town for the Samsung 500. In June, IndyCars show their stuff at the Bombardier Learjet 550, and NASCAR returns in November with its year-ending Chase for the Cup at the AAA 500. In just a decade, Texas Motor Speedway has become one of the premier tracks in auto racing, producing such winners as Dale Earnhardt Jr., Tony Stewart and Al Unser Jr.

SHOPPING

The Best Hat Store
2739 North Main Street
Fort Worth, Texas
817-625-6650

Keith and Susan Maddox opened the Best Hat Store to bring to Fort Worth and the north Texas area a superior selection of brands, colors, quality and fit in western hats. Keith is a thirty-year veteran of the western wear industry, and Susan brings twenty-one years experience in the retail sales to the business. From a modest beginning, with about 1,500 hats in stock, the Best Hat Store has grown to become one of the country's leading specialty hat stores. It now maintains a year-round inventory of more than 4,000 hats, including more than one hundred different styles in felt hats alone.

Bum Steer
2400 North Main Street
Fort Worth, Texas
817-626-4565

A visit to this store can be a real adventure into the world of Texas and the Old West. Offering western furniture and accessories, there is a hint of western adventure including antler chandeliers and iron candleholders.

The Crosseyed Moose
2322 North Main Street
Fort Worth, Texas
817-624-4311

Specializing in cowboy and Old West décor, the Crosseyed Moose also sells upscale western furniture and features western memorabilia, rustic tables and chairs, elegant yet rugged desks and other western furnishings.

Ernest Tubb Record Shop
817-624-8449

Founded by the famous Ernest Tubb, this record shop has been filling country music fans' needs for more than fifty-nine years. Everything you need in country music is offered, from past and present: records, tapes, CDs, videos and memorabilia.

Fincher's White Front Western Wear
115 East Exchange Avenue
Fort Worth, Texas
817.624.7302

Fincher's White Front Western Wear is located in the heart of the historic Fort Worth Stockyards in a huge, white, two-story building, with a rust horse mannequin outside. In operation since 1902, Fincher's stocks a full line of western wear, from infant to adults.

The Front Porch
2515 Rodeo Plaza
Fort Worth, Texas
817-626-3000

Roger and Vickie Francis offer an array of sand candles, some shaped like the state of Texas, hearts and crescent moons in a variety of sizes. Having taught himself to carve ivory in 1975, Roger Francis has gained acclaim as one of the finest ivory carvers in the United States. He makes his carvings from prehistoric woolly mammoth ivory, mastodon ivory or fossilized walrus teeth. Roger has won many awards through the years, including Best of Show awards at the Texas State Fair. In 1976, he carved matching ivory wing pendants for Paul and Linda McCartney. Some of the other people he has created his designs for include former president Ronald Reagan, Mick Jagger, Willie Nelson, the Grateful Dead's Jerry Garcia, Jimmy Buffet, James Taylor, Stevie Nicks, Joe Walsh, Glen Tilbrook and the Smothers Brothers (Tom and Dick).

Leather Trading Company
140 East Exchange Avenue, #125
Fort Worth, Texas
817-624-4993

A good line of Texas-inspired clothing and accessories is sold here.

Longhorn General Store
130 East Exchange Avenue
Fort Worth, Texas 76164
817-625-9715

Blue Bell Ice Cream and Dublin Dr. Pepper—now that's Texas! Here there are also T-shirts, personalized collectibles, cowboy ropes and spurs.

Maverick Fine Western Wear
100 East Exchange Avenue
Fort Worth, Texas
800-282-1315

Maverick Fine Western Wear, established in 1987, is located in the historic Fort Worth Stockyards in a building from 1905. In addition to the shopping, there is also a bar reminiscent of the good old days of the big cattle drives. It also carries a wide variety of products that enhance the western lifestyle, features most of the top brands in men's and women's apparel, has its own label on the finest quality of custom-made hats, boots and jewelry and sells the finest in leather and fur coats for men and women.

M.L. Leddy's Boots & Saddlery
2455 North Main Street
Fort Worth, Texas
888-565-2668

Makers of custom hats, clothing, boots and saddles—completely handmade from start to finish, using the finest materials available, by craftsmen who through years of experience are truly experts in their field.

Old Tyme Mercantile
817-625-1822

Old Thyme Mercantile offers authentic historical clothing, hats and leather goods of the Old West and the American Civil War, as well as an assortment of western collectibles.

Ponder Boot Company
2358 North Main Street
Fort Worth, Texas
817-626-0089

Ponder Boot offers custom handmade fine leather creations: exotic hide leather boots, belts, shoes, purses, custom alligator golf page and briefcases. It makes the items from a wide selection of fine leathers or exotic hides, as well as ordinary leathers. All of its products are offered in any color or combination of colors, and products are designed by the customers to suit their individual needs. Ponder Boot began in Ponder, Texas, in the late 1970s in the bank building, forever recognized in history by the attempt of Bonnie and Clyde to rob their first bank in the 1930s.

Roy Earl's Metal Art
2501 Rodeo Plaza
Fort Worth, Texas
817-626-0066

Metal art with a Texas flair. Roy Earl and Maricela have been at the historic Fort Worth Stockyards in the Rodeo Plaza for years. They offer handmade western décor and jewelry and can also do custom orders.

Sean Ryon Western Store & Saddle Shop
2707 North Main Street
Fort Worth, Texas
817-626-2440

Sean Ryon's family has worked in the Fort Worth Stockyards for more than a century. T.J. Ryon moved there in the late 1800s as a cattle buyer and had a ranch where Meacham Airport is now located. Marine Creek Lake was part of his ranch, the last watering hole before the cattle came into the Stockyards. T.J.'s son, Don, was an auctioneer, appropriately nicknamed "Windy." His son, Don Jr., known as "Little Windy," opened the original Ryon Western Store in the Fort Worth Livestock Exchange Building in 1944 and eventually relocated to Main Street. Don Ryon III, nicknamed "Whistle," Sean's father, continued the family business and then sold to Charles Tandy in 1978. In 1989, Sean reestablished the family business, opening the Sean Ryon Western Store & Saddle Shop.

The Spice & Tea Exchange
817-626-2300

Customers can enjoy and open the more than two hundred hand-blown glass jars on the walls and smell the freshness of the spices, loose teas, sea salts and the hand-mixed blends made in the store. You can also find great rubs for steaks, pork, chicken and seafood, and there is an assortment of fragrant and unique loose teas. The sea salts come from around the world and feature smoked and mineral salts, and there are also accessories to be found, starting with western cutting boards in the shape of longhorn steers, the state of Texas and horse heads.

Stockyards Trading Post
817-624-4424

This business sells hats, western accessories and a ton of Texas collectibles.

Stockyards Wines
817-625-5880

Wines from all over Texas are sold by the glass or bottle.

Tattoo Ranch
108 West Exchange Avenue
Fort Worth, Texas
817-626-7400

With some of the area's most talented tattoo artists, it seems appropriate in its Old World charm and is noted as the "most upscale, historical tattoo studio in North Texas."

Texas Hot Stuff
817-625-1221

Texas Hot Stuff can help you gauge the amount of heat you can handle with a huge assortment of Texas-style zesty sauces and marinades, while also offering western home décor including cowhides, picture frames, candles, birdhouses and homemade fudge.

Annual Festivals and Events in Fort Worth

Southwestern Exposition and Livestock Show & Rodeo (January–February)
http://www.fwssr.com

Established in 1896, this popular event attracts nearly 1 million people from around the world to the Will Rogers Memorial Center for the nation's oldest livestock show and daily performances of the world's original indoor rodeo.

Cowboys of Color Rodeo (January)
www.cowboysofcolor.org

The rodeos are a wonderful way to bring families together to experience collective western heritage and to acknowledge multiple contributions by diverse cultures. This event is held during the Fort Worth Stock Show and Rodeo in the Will Rogers Coliseum.

The Last Great Gunfight (February)
www.stockyardsstation.com

Historic Stockyards outside White Elephant Saloon, described in an earlier section.

Cowtown Marathon (February)
www.cowtownmarathon.org

The race begins in Sundance Square and laces through Fort Worth neighborhoods.

Race Week at Texas Motor Speedway (April, June, and November)
Texas Motor Speedway
http://www.texasmotorspeedway.com

Three times a year, Texas Motor Speedway hosts NASCAR and IndyCar racing events.

Main Street Fort Worth Arts Festival (April)
www.mainstreetartsfest.org

Nine blocks of Fort Worth's historic brick-paved Main Street become a marketplace of food, arts, crafts and live entertainment during this popular annual festival.

Texas Frontier Forts Day (May)

www.stockyardsstation.com

During this free two-day heritage event, the Stockyards National Historic District is transformed into an authentic representation of Texas frontier life.

Mayfest (May)

www.fortworthgov.org

A family festival featuring food, arts, crafts and live performances, held on the banks of the Trinity River.

National Tourism Week (May)

www.ustravel.org

National Tourism Week is a collective effort to promote the power of travel through customized events in communities nationwide. The goal is to enhance the country's economy, security and perception and recognize the cultural and social benefits created by travel and tourism.

Crowne Plaza Invitational at Colonial Country Club (May)

www.colonialfw.com

One of professional golf's classic tournaments, this nationally televised competition features the nation's top golfers on the PGA tour at Fort Worth's prestigious Colonial Country Club.

Fort Worth Opera Festival (May–June)

www.fwopera.org

The Fort Worth Opera decided to try an opera festival format, instead of the traditional fall/winter season, so that an entire season's worth of operas could be performed in a matter of weeks.

Van Cliburn International Piano Competition (May–June)
www.cliburn.org

Every four years, Fort Worth becomes "the Mecca of classical music," according to the *Boston Globe*. Thirty of today's most promising pianists gather to reveal their immense talents.

Juneteenth Celebration (June)
www.juneteenth.com

The celebration includes a parade in downtown Fort Worth and daylong activities near the Fort Worth Convention Center.

Fort Worth Symphony Orchestra's Concerts in the Garden (June–July)
www.fwsymphony.org

The concerts include evening performances by the Fort Worth Symphony Orchestra and special guest artists, staged outdoors in the Fort Worth Botanic Garden. All performances conclude with a fireworks finale.

National Day of the American Cowboy (July)
www.cowboyday.com

A celebration of the American cowboy.

Jazz By the Boulevard Festival (September)
www.campbowiedistrict.com

Celebrate Fort Worth's rich musical heritage with live performances of all types of jazz, from classic and big band to hot Latin beats and rhythm-and-blues. There are also cultural exhibits, interactive workshops, dance performances and a showcase of Camp Bowie retailers and professional fine artists.

Fort Worth Alliance Airshow (October)
www.allianceairshow.com

The Fort Worth Alliance Air Show is one of the nation's premier air shows, drawing the best in aviation talent, static displays and ground activities.

MusicArte de Fort Worth (October)

An exciting and colorful celebration of Latino cultures, featuring entertainment, dance, art, food and fun.

Boo at the Zoo (October)
www.fortworthzoo.com

This not-too-scary family event is complete with live entertainment, games, costumed characters and trick-or-treating.

Red Steagall Cowboy Gathering & Western Swing Festival (October)
www.redsteagallcowboygathering.com

This is one of the top authentic cowboy festivals in the world. Music, ranch rodeo, cowboy poetry and more come together to celebrate the heritage of the American cowboy.

Lone Star International Film Festival (November)
www.lsiff.com

The Lone Star International Film Festival, hosted by the Lone Star Film Society, is a year-round series of programs, culminating in a five-day celebration of cinema in mid-November. The festival's purpose is to showcase artistically and culturally significant films and provide educational forums through which filmmakers and enthusiasts can learn more about the art and business of cinema.

Chesapeake Energy Parade of Lights presented by CHASE
(November)
www.sundancesquare.com

This spectacularly illuminated holiday parade features decorative floats, horses, carriages, marching bands and more, ending with the lighting of the Fort Worth Christmas tree downtown.

Christmas in the Stockyards (December)
www.stockyardsstation.com

Here we have full-day Christmas events, including family and children's activities, a petting zoo, the Fort Worth Herd "CowKid Round-up," "Ride for Toys" on horseback, Christmas tree lighting, carolers, Santa Claus, vendors and much more.

Bell Helicopter Armed Forces Bowl (December)
www.espn.com

The Bell Helicopter Armed Forces Bowl, owned and operated by ESPN Regional Television (ERT), is televised live annually from Amon G. Carter Stadium.

BIBLIOGRAPHY

Bureau of Engraving and Printing. "Fort Worth Location." http://www.moneyfactory.gov/tours/fortworthtxtours.html.

Cashion, Ty. *The New Frontier: A Contemporary History of Fort Worth and Tarrant County.* Fort Worth, TX: Fort Worth Stockyards Business Association, 2006.

Fort Worth Convention and Visitors Bureau. http://www.fortworth.com.

The Fort Worth Stock Show and Rodeo. http://www.fwssr.com.

The Fort Worth Stockyards. http://www.fortworthstockyards.org.

Historic Fort Worth, Inc. http://www.historicfortworth.org/Home/tabid/55/Default.aspx.

Log Cabin Village. http://www.logcabinvillage.org.

Miss Molly's Hotel. http://www.missmollyshotel.com.

National Register of Historic Places. "The Fort Worth Botanic Garden." http://www.nps.gov/history/nr/feature/landscape/2010/fort_worth_botanic_garden.htm.

BIBLIOGRAPHY

Stockyards Museum. http://www.stockyardsmuseum.org.

Stopping Points.com. "City of Fort Worth Historical Markers." http://www.stoppingpoints.com/texas/city.cgi?city=Fort+Worth&cnty=tarrant.

Texas Historical Commission. "Texas Historic Landmarks." http://www.thc.state.tx.us/aboutus/abtdefault.shtml.

Whitington, Mitchel. *Ghosts of North Texas.* Lanham, MD: A Republic of Texas Press Book, 2003.

Wikipedia. "People of note from Fort Worth, Texas." http://en.wikipedia.org/wiki/List_of_people_from_Fort_Worth,_Texas.

INDEX

ABOUT THE AUTHOR

Rita Cook is a writer/editor who has more than one thousand articles to her credit in the past thirteen or more years. She is a frequent auto and travel contributor on a radio show in Los Angeles called *Insider Mag Radio* at KPRO 1570 am, on from midnight to 12:30 a.m. Monday mornings. She is also the editor in chief of *Insider Mag*. Cook is a member of the Texas Auto Writer's Association, writes for the *Dallas Morning News*' "Green Living" section in addition to artist profiles and has an auto column with the *Washington Times*' "Communities" section. Spending much of her time on the road, traveling or working on books, this is Cook's fifth bylined book; she has also ghostwritten numerous others. Married, Cook lives in the Dallas/Fort Worth area.

Visit us at
www.historypress.net